REMEMBERING

JOHNSON CITY

REMEMBERING

JOHNSON CITY

BOB L. COX

Charleston   London

THE
History
PRESS

Published by The History Press
Charleston, SC 29403
www.historypress.net

Cover design by Natasha Momberger

First published 2008

Manufactured in the United States

ISBN 978.1.59629.483.7

Library of Congress Cataloging-in-Publication Data

Cox, Bob L.
Remembering Johnson City / Bob L. Cox.
p. cm.
Includes bibliographical references.
ISBN 978-1-59629-483-7
1. Johnson City (Tenn.)--History--Anecdotes. 2. Johnson City (Tenn.)--Social life and customs--Anecdotes. I. Title.
F444.J67C69 2008
976.8'97--dc22

2008033423

CONTENTS

PREFACE

Throughout its colorful and storied past, Johnson City in Northeast Tennessee has evolved through four names—Johnson's Tank, Johnson's Depot, Haynesville and, finally, Johnson City. In addition, it has carried myriad impressive descriptors, including "the Coming City of the South," "the Switzerland of America," "the City of Progress and Prosperity," "Gateway of the Appalachians" and "the Hub of Upper East Tennessee," and it was once envisioned as the future "Pittsburgh of the South."

The mountainous municipality is located in Washington County, the oldest and first settled region in the state. It was here, in 1771, that a colony became the first free and independent government, acquiring the name of Watauga Association.

At one time, Johnson City was traversed by five railroads: the Southern (originally the East Tennessee, Virginia and Georgia); Carolina, Clinchfield and Ohio (CC&O); East Tennessee and Western North Carolina (ET&WNC); Virginia and Southwestern; and the Johnson City Southern (Embreeville extension of the Southern). A sixth line, the Carolina, Cincinnati and Chicago (3Cs) Railway almost became a reality, but unfavorable economic conditions shut it down before it became operable. The railroad town is located about one hundred miles northeast of Knoxville and about twenty-five miles from both the Virginia and North Carolina state lines. Over its long history, which commenced in 1869, the city's population increased from 637 to 4,150 within a single decade, and it more than doubled by 1910, making it the third largest town in Northeast Tennessee.

Johnson City is situated at 1,650 feet above sea level in the foothills of what was formerly referred to as the Southern Allegheny mountain range, now known as the Appalachians. These majestic mountains, with several subsidiary ranges, are in full view of the city; the closest is

Buffalo Mountain, a part of the Cherokee National Forest to the south. Located about fifty miles from the Appalachian Trail, Johnson City shares approximately the same scenery and climate with nearby Asheville, North Carolina. The region is particularly noted for its cool summer nights and freedom from malaria, mosquitoes and epidemics. Protected by the Appalachian Mountains on the east and the Cumberland Mountains on the west, the city encounters relatively few destructive winds. The altitude makes summer temperatures much lower and more comfortable than those recorded in cities to its north.

Within an hour's train ride from "the Switzerland of America" were once located some of the most celebrated summer resorts in the country. The Cloudland Hotel, on the top of Roan Mountain, was the highest habitable point east of the Rocky Mountains (elevation 6,300 feet). It was a notable haven for sufferers of hay fever and malarial troubles, and a place patronized frequently by Johnson Citians, who made the remote trip by rail. Another trendy resort was at Linville, North Carolina, located near the foot of Grandfather Mountain (elevation 5,000 feet). Unaka Springs, twenty miles distant and situated at the foot of several towering peaks on the banks of the Nolachucky River, was recognized for its medicinal spring. Other nearby areas included Austin Springs and King Springs, whose waters are principally chalybeate and lithia.

Having been born and raised in Johnson City, I attended several city schools: West Side, Henry Johnson, Junior High, Science Hill High and East Tennessee State University. This book presents the city's historical past using an assortment of information from school annuals, city directories, newspaper clippings, history books and interviews of individuals. Many of the people who possessed firsthand knowledge of the subject matter are now deceased.

The topics in this book include a brief history of a great land in Northeast Tennessee; a glance at how the city evolved into what it is today; an examination of the humble and restrained individual whose name is identified with the city; recognition of businesses that significantly contributed to the success of the town; a beautiful bronze statue that once graced downtown Fountain Square, ended up in North Carolina for several years and then majestically returned to the city a few years later; the elephant that misbehaved and found itself dangling at the end of a rail yard gallows; a man whose first ride in a motor vehicle was while being escorted in an ambulance to the hospital; the youngster whose gravel-flipping skills made him the envy of the community; the record collector who longed for more songs to be written about Johnson City; a debating society that developed into the city's main high school; two local boys who became Tennessee governors and who proudly claimed to be fiddlers, not violinists; the excitement of experiencing the popular John Robinson Circus on its annual trek to the city; a caring mother honored by a club in New York City for raising thirteen boys; a county fair with humble beginnings that later became an annual major attraction; a newspaper headline that shocked and saddened the populace with the dreaded words, "Our Bob Is Dead"; trailblazer Daniel Boone, who literally left his mark upon Northeast Tennessee; and the diminutive Johnson's Depot, which grew into a five-railroad town.

I wish to thank my cousin, Dr. James Bowman, for perusing my manuscript and offering numerous helpful suggestions. I am appreciative of Norma Myers, director of the East Tennessee State University's Archives of Appalachia, and her helpful and affable staff for their valuable and timely assistance. I was permitted to research countless archive collections of text and photographs, several of which are displayed in this book. I am grateful to Glenn K. Berry, who snapped the photograph that graces the front and back covers of this book; Alan Bridwell, webmaster of the award-winning www.johnsonsdepot.com, who assisted me during my research; and Clarence Greene, for sharing memories and photos of his famous father, who recorded "Johnson City Blues" for Columbia Records in the city in 1928.

Sit back and enjoy a comfortable and hopefully pleasant excursion down memory lane in the expansive region centered at beautiful Johnson City, Tennessee.

A BRIEF HISTORY OF A
BEAUTIFUL, MOUNTAINOUS LAND

In the mid-1800s, a large tract of land nestled deep in the magnificent Blue Ridge Mountains of Northeast Tennessee lay nearly barren, begging to be discovered by fortunate settlers. A handful of venturesome pioneers heeded that distant call, one of whom was Henry Johnson, a resident of Western North Carolina. He wandered upon the stunningly picturesque area that would later bear his name with enough energy and drive to transform a quaint, diminutive village into a bustling railroad town and later into a large city that was branded "the Switzerland of America."

Outside the towering wall of rolling hills and tranquil mountains, few people were aware of the area's natural resources and scenic splendor. Since the early years, modern civilization had seemingly fallen in love with East Tennessee and thoroughly penetrated the region, denting somewhat, but not marring, its rustic charm. Quickly recognizing the many advantages of this Southern mountain locale, industrial capitalists methodically began replacing Native American land with sprawling manufactories. The sharp contrast between Southern graciousness and mountain roughness was suddenly apparent.

The fog-shrouded Great Smoky Mountains dominate the horizon of Northeast Tennessee and Western North Carolina. In 1934, a section of the region became a major national park, embracing some of the country's oldest mountains covered in virgin forests replete with large bark-wood trees. At 6,593 feet, the park contains the second-highest mountain peak, from the base to the summit, east of the Mississippi River.

Early records show that a few families, as far back as 1771, populated the territory of present-day Johnson City. The small number of scattered folks squatted on land along Brush Creek, in an area first identified as "South Watauga" because it was situated south of the Watauga River. A state historical marker (1A 89), located near the intersection of West Watauga Avenue and Jackson Avenue, contains the words:

> *On September 2, 1811, James Nelson deeded to trustees William Nelson, William Duzan, James King, Jacob Hoss and John R. Boring, 4 acres and 8 poles to be used by the Methodist Episcopal Church for a house of worship. For many years a campground for religious meetings was maintained here with a central permanent test and many family tents. During the Civil War Col. Robert Loves' 62nd N.C. Regiment, CSA, used the ground as a camp.*

This stretch of land would assume other names over the years, including Brush Creek, Blue Plum, Johnson's Tank, Johnson's Depot and Haynesville, before being chartered as Johnson City on December 1, 1869. To the west, on Brush Creek, Robert Young Sr. and his sons—Robert Jr., Charles, Thomas, William and Joseph—settled on property that later became the location of the Veterans Administration, East Tennessee State University and the Quillen College of Medicine. To the east, Jonas Little, George Little, Benjamin Denton and William Ward took up land. There were a few other early families present: Robertsons, McMahons, Fains, Jonathan Tipton, Jeremiah Dungan and Peter Range, all with residences some distance from the downtown area. From 1782 until 1792, a host of Virginia and North Carolina families settled in this location. Among them were Hosses, Humphreys, Kings and Darling Jones. The name "South Watauga" continued unofficially until about 1805, when James Nelson, son of William, gave "four acres and four poles" on Brush Creek to the Methodist Society (Bishop Francis Asbury) for the purpose of establishing a church, which was also used for educational purposes.

The Boones Creek section to the north of Johnson City was named for Daniel Boone (Boon), American pioneer and trailblazer who became one of the truly great folk heroes of American history. The legendary figure, known for his bold exploration in dense expanses heavily populated with Indians, began a winter hunt in 1760, when he was only twenty-six years old. This journey brought him from the Yadkin River in North Carolina west to the Blue Ridge Mountains of Virginia. Boone was highly impressed with the paradise he encountered, consisting of fertile farmland and a wide variety of wild game—buffalo, wild turkey, deer, opossum, raccoon, squirrel, fox, rabbit, quail, pigeon, dove and numerous other birds. Buffalo were the first civil engineers in the region, pounding out early roads with their heavy weight as they moved around.

It is easy to see why Native Americans and early pioneers found Tennessee country so inviting. Boone later informed his family members of his desire to one day permanently reside in the region. As with any folk hero from our

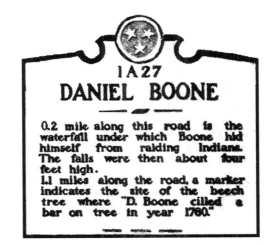

The Daniel Boone Tennessee State Historical Marker that once stood in Gray Station, just down the road from the old Boones Creek High School. *Courtesy of the Bob Cox Collection.*

history, Boone's story is likely a mixture of fact and fiction. The folklore hero once humorously commented about the thick undergrowth: "I have never been lost, but I will admit to being confused for several weeks."

A Tennessee state historical marker (1A 27) in Boones Creek, near Johnson City, once encapsulated two facts about the pioneer's brief stopover in Northeast Tennessee during the journey. The sign stood along Gray Station Road, a short distance from old Boones Creek High School:

> *0.2 mile along this road is the waterfall under which Boone hid himself from raiding Indians; the falls were then about 4 ft. high. 1.1 miles along the road, a marker indicates the site of the beech tree where "D. Boon cilled a bar in year 1760."*

Two photos of the waterfalls are known to exist, one showing the falls as they appeared around the turn of the century, and the other taken about 1957. The height of the falls is significantly reduced between the two pictures. While those in the latter one appear to be too small for a person to hide behind, the older one reveals that the falls were large enough then for a person to go under and be fully concealed. Legend has it that while Boone was on a hunting trip, he encountered several Cherokee Indians, who immediately began chasing him. In an attempt to prevent them from discovering the location of his camp, the wily trailblazer momentarily distanced himself from his pursuers and simultaneously spotted a nearby waterfall. Quick thinking caused him to climb through the curtain of water and hide beneath a ledge without being noticed. The Indians were mystified

The famous large beech tree that contained Daniel Boone's carved initials. The trailblazer trekked through the Johnson City area in 1760. *Courtesy of the Archives of Appalachia, East Tennessee State University, Pat Watson Collection.*

by his sudden disappearance and lack of visible tracks. Allegedly, after several minutes, the superstitious natives became frightened and ran away, thinking that Boone had turned into an invisible spirit.

The second piece of information on the historical marker refers to an American beech tree (*Fagus grandifolia*) that was said to stand in sight of, and to the east of, "the present stage road that leads from Jonesboro [now Jonesborough] to Blountsville [now Blountville] and in the valley of Boon's Creek, a tributary of Watauga." It is generally accepted that the 26-year-old pioneer etched this carving during his Northeast Tennessee sojourn. One theory suggests that it was one of Boone's acquaintances who actually made the carving. Another report estimates that the tree was 365 years old and had a girth of twenty-eight and a half feet. Beech trees have long been popular with sweethearts who carve their initials in the smooth, gray bark. Boone was simply perpetuating an ancient custom of leaving a message behind on a tree with no thought of defacement. Daniel's last name is spelled "Boon," not "Boone." The tree's inscription remained legible until about 1880. Fortunately, the carved area was photographed before it faded into nonexistence. The big tree fell about 1916 during an electrical storm. City officials salvaged the wood and used it to fabricate gavels for souvenirs and to be distributed as gifts to visiting dignitaries.

A Brief History of a Beautiful, Mountainous Land

Washington County became home to other notables—Davy Crockett, Andrew Jackson, Andrew Johnson, John Sevier and Samuel Doak. In 1780, Doak, a Presbyterian minister and Princeton graduate, founded Washington College, the first school established west of the Alleghenies. It is located about ten miles from Johnson City. George Washington was said to have approved the use of his name for the school. Another important nearby site is Sycamore Shoals, the location of Fort Watauga, just outside of Elizabethton, where the Overmountain Men organized in 1780 in preparation to trek over the Blue Ridge Mountains at Roan Mountain to King's Mountain, South Carolina, to defeat British Major Patrick Ferguson.

A significant time in Johnson City's storied past occurred when the city became a boomtown during the 1880s. Its attractive location, scenic splendor and strategic potentialities were duly noted by pioneer builder John T. Wilder, who is credited with helping ignite the city's economic growth, calling the world's attention to what many believed to be the fairest spot on the face of the earth. But, like many towns that experienced booms, greedy speculators soon caused land prices to become so inflated that holders could not meet financial obligations, resulting in collapse. Although the severe blow momentarily destroyed confidence in the city's future, its plentiful resources and flourishing opportunities were simply too great for it to lie dormant for any length of time. After recovering from those disappointing years, Johnson City became one of the most important commercial and manufacturing centers within a radius of one hundred miles.

Despite the crash of the 1880s, three competing trunk lines entered the city, providing not only cheap freight rates to all points, but also ensuring cheap coal, thus securing for manufacturers a permanent and unfailing fuel supply. The nearby Nolachucky, Watauga and Holston Rivers afforded crucial power sites. The surrounding deposits of minerals, the great variety and supply of hardwoods and cheap and abundant labor truly made Johnson City well positioned to handle the needs of the future.

A 1911 city directory offers a hint of the many advantages the city held for citizens and businessmen that year. It further emphasized that natural advantages do not always make an ideal city; the municipal advantages must be adequate as well. The directory noted that the needs of Johnson City were being looked after by a farseeing, capable and intelligent group of businessmen, who realized the city's potential, were aware of its phenomenal growth and expected future increases. These farsighted individuals were making plans for the great influx of people soon to arrive in the city by laying the groundwork for a modern, up-to-date municipality. Specific projects included a new federal building, erection of a Union Passenger depot at

This postcard from about 1908 depicts Main Street looking east from Fountain Square. The downtown area sported a new look, with bricked streets and paved sidewalks. Note the trolley tracks in the middle of the street. *Courtesy of the Bob Cox Collection.*

JOHNSON CITY, TENN.

CITY DIRECTORY

Vol. III	**1911**	Vol. III

THE PIEDMONT SERIES.

" THE COMING CITY OF THE SOUTH "

JOHNSON CITY, TENN. Address Your Communications to THE COMMERCIAL CLUB

A 1911 City Directory identified Johnson City as "the Coming City of the South" because of the many business opportunities it afforded. *Courtesy of the Archives of Appalachia, East Tennessee State University.*

a cost of $100,000; a modern sewer and water system; brick streets and several miles of concrete sidewalks; additional banks; an expanded education system; elegant, costly church edifices; and the building of numerous new retail stores and modern residences. These dedicated planners would spare nothing to make their city great. The "Coming City of the South" was starting to earn its name.

HENRY JOHNSON:

JOHNSON CITY'S

UNPRETENTIOUS FOUNDER

The beginning of Johnson City can be traced back to 1856, when a hardy pioneer, Henry Johnson, who was reportedly as humble as the little township he founded, traveled through the East Tennessee region and became enamored with what he found. This was about one hundred years after Daniel Boone forged this same area. While other residents were present about this time, it was Johnson who grabbed the reins of progress and methodically drove the quaint little village toward the thriving metropolis that it is today. His story is an impressive one.

Although Johnson made no effort to venerate his name by using it to establish a city, there are many personal traits that reveal that he possessed a productive, farseeing, unselfish character that focused on community building, rapid growth and progressive development. The increase in population of this segment of the Appalachian range evolved as remote wildernesses began transforming into centers of highest civilization, almost within the span of one generation.

The facts surrounding Henry Johnson, the man, have become somewhat blurred with time and scarcity of documentation. He was born in 1809 in North Carolina, most likely in the western half of the state. He obviously had some formal education because there is evidence that he used proper English, expressed himself well and possessed excellent penmanship. Although he focused his efforts on matters pertaining to the welfare of the community, he managed to take time for such recreational activities as playing checkers and fishing with friends. He often brought home a mess of fish caught in nearby Brush Creek. The founder was known to possess Christian virtues that resulted in his taking an unyielding stand on the teachings of the church.

There is speculation that Henry and Andrew Johnson, the seventeenth president of the United States, were related, the reason being that both men

The only photo known to exist of Johnson City's founder, Henry Johnson, extracted from an old "tin-type" plate. *Courtesy of Betty Jane Hylton.*

lived in the same section of the country at a time when it was sparsely populated. Henry, like Andrew, who became known as "the Great Commoner," was tall and big-boned, as were all the Anglo-Saxons who settled in East Tennessee and Western North Carolina around the time of the Revolutionary War. These people, whose ancestors established the first independent form of government on the North American continent, were quiet, hardy, slender, discerning and even jealous of their own powers and abilities. On February 23, 1834, Henry married Mary Ann Hoss, daughter of John Hoss, who was a grandnephew of Daniel Boone, in North Carolina. The couple had five children—three sons and two daughters. One of the daughters died in infancy; the other married and became the mother of a large family. A son, John Johnson, was a young soldier during the Civil War.

When Henry Johnson arrived in the Johnson City area in 1856, he built a combination residence and merchant store on what is now the southwest side of West Market Street at the Southern Railroad tracks. Although there were four or five other houses in the vicinity, this is believed to have been the first business establishment in the town. One of the neighboring residences

Henry Johnson: Johnson City's Unpretentious Founder

Henry Johnson's first structure was a combination residence and merchant store. The building became a hotel that accommodated travelers on Old Stage Road (later renamed Market Street). *Courtesy of the Archives of Appalachia, East Tennessee State University, Burr Harrison Collection.*

was owned by Tipton Jobe and faced north at the present southwest corner of Tipton and Spring Streets. The front yard extended across Tipton Street to Main Street at Fountain Square, on property that would later house Jobe's Opera House. Photos of Johnson, or his home, store, hotel and depot, are scarce, but thanks to two of Johnson's relatives—Mrs. Fred Artz, a niece, and Mrs. Minnie Pickens, a granddaughter—a few old pictures of the Johnson era were preserved. The only photo of Henry known to exist is an enlarged image from an old "tin-type" plate that appears to have been taken in his prime.

Other nearby residences included some that were considered to be "in the country" at the time. A few were already present when Johnson arrived, and others were built about the time of his sojourn, including the Abram Hoss house, located immediately north of the old Southern Railway freight depot; the T.J. Faw property, the site of the future John Sevier Hotel; the Bowman home to the south of the city; and the Caruthers Farm in the western edge of the city, near what is now referred to as Cherokee Heights. Johnson's home and store were located on what was then known as the Old Stage Road, which extended from North Carolina, through this section of town, to Knoxville, with a branch of it going into Virginia and on toward the west.

In all probability, Henry came over this dirt road by means of the usual conveyances of the day, the covered wagon. There were no rail connections to Western North Carolina because the East Tennessee and Virginia Railroad was not yet in operation. This railroad later merged with the East Tennessee and Georgia Railroad to become the East Tennessee, Virginia and Georgia Railroad, later acquiring the name Southern Railway. Early in 1857, trains were operating from Bristol to Johnson's Tank. Railroad management initially considered Johnson's quaint little town to be too inconsequential to justify stopping there, except for taking on water. After Henry became aware of this fact, he vowed to increase the town's significance in order to make it a viable railroad stop. His relentless labor for that cause would prove to be successful.

When the city founder built his brick house, the lower floor was used as a storeroom, handling the general line of merchandise of the day: from millinery to mousetraps, hardware to eggs and bar lead to bullet molds. Those were the days when "medicinal" beverages were sold over the counter, not as contraband, but as a regular commodity, serving as a reminder of the time when a gallon of rum was used as a standard monetary unit.

The Johnson home not only served as his family's residence, but it also became a hotel for the accommodation of trekkers on the Old Stage Road. Travelers would often time their excursions so as to make it to the Johnson hotel by sundown. Legend has it that Henry never refused a weary or hungry voyager in need of a hot meal and a good night's lodging. If the unfortunate individual could pay his bill, that was fine. If he needed to pay his debt in produce or animal hides, that was also acceptable. If he was broke and unable to shell out money for the tab, that too was deemed satisfactory. Such a spirit of hospitality vividly displayed the underlying decent fabric of Henry Johnson. The nearest "neighbor" at that time was the railroad water tank to the south of his property, located across from Fountain Square on land that became known as "Rotary Park," in front of and across the tracks from the Windsor Hotel.

Johnson next built a wooden train depot at his own expense along the railroad tracks in the middle of the block between Main and Market Streets. The building was used as a combination freight and passenger station, express office, warehouse, waiting room and, eventually, telegraph station. Henry became depot, freight, ticket and express agents, plus anything else related to the venture. Later, he built a second station, fabricated of brick, just south of the old one on land that, in time, became the site of the Arlington and Fountain Square hotels. The Western Union Telegraph Company office was built near the water tank on land later used for the city

Henry Johnson: Johnson City's Unpretentious Founder

Henry Johnson's wooden train depot, built at his own expense. It was located along the railroad tracks in the middle of the block between Main and Market Streets. *Courtesy of the Archives of Appalachia, East Tennessee State University, Burr Harrison Collection.*

bus terminal at Buffalo and Main. This action, he believed, would enhance the development of the small village. He was right; Johnson's Depot, which began as the name of the train station, soon became the designation of the small but growing town. Good things were on the horizon. The little village was about to explode in population.

Reportedly, the village initially became known as Johnson's Tank by envious Jonesboro residents, who saw the small town's population increasing rapidly. The nearby land at that time was attractive because it was not rough wilderness or virgin forest. Jonesboro had been established a half century earlier, and the section that included the present business portion of Johnson City had been "entered" by Abraham Jobe nearly seventy years earlier. Settlers had purchased it from North Carolina before Tennessee came into existence, and it was known as "Washington County, North Carolina." Johnson purchased the tract on which he built his dwelling from Tipton Jobe as part of his plantation.

Henry Johnson was known to be an energetic man and was constantly active in some meaningful project involving city development. He wore no gaudy clothing, but instead chose more unassuming garments. However, he cared about his appearance; his vesture had to be of good material and immaculate in semblance. Those who were personally acquainted with the city's namesake recalled that he wore his customary long, black coat, greased his boots regularly, put on a high, uncomfortable collar and wore a necktie, usually on Sunday. He was described as being a man of little wit who took everything seriously, which opened the way for his being the brunt of practical jokes and pranks by those of the younger generation.

Henry made a strategic move by petitioning to have the post office moved from Blue Plum, two miles south of the depot, to a partitioned area at the rear of his store, where he became postmaster. When parcels arrived by train, he opened the big mail pouch, emptied it onto a table and called out, in a voice described as being a mezzo tenor, the names of the addresses to a nearby crowd of anxious bystanders waiting to find out if they had received any correspondence from the train. Those fortunate recipients of parcels were required to answer "present" in an audible voice and then quickly come to the window to obtain their items. If the addressee was not present, Henry usually asked someone to take the mail to the person. Those were the days when people readily assisted their friends.

Young men in the crowd frequently engaged in merriment by answering "present" for some absent person whose name was called. The wily postmaster, not to be fooled by their pranks, had little difficulty in recognizing the feigned voice. He did not hesitate to berate the guilty offenders with such comments as: "I guarantee you are interfering with the United States mail and if you don't stop, I'll have the law on you." Court records do not reveal that the threat was met with a severe sentence for the "crime." When a latecomer drifted in after the mail was opened and distributed and asked for his mail, Johnson would berate him or her for not being on hand at the prescribed time. His punishment was to make the "offender" wait until he reached a convenient stopping place, even if he was engaged in a serious game of checkers.

Those individuals who knew Henry Johnson recall that he secured the greater part of the firewood used in his dwelling and hotel from neighboring farms, largely from boys who would haul in a load for fifteen or twenty cents and gladly receive their compensation in gumdrops, licorice or chewing tobacco from the store.

Records do not specify that Johnson possessed any significant material wealth or owned large plots of land; his real estate holdings seemed to be confined to the comparatively small amount of property on which his home and business were located. He acquired the reputation of being a shrewd businessman in his mercantile ventures and later built two or three additional houses on his property. One of his noble passions was promoting quality education for village youth.

Henry's independence of action was demonstrated by an incident pertaining to his depot. He made a request to the railroad company that was not complied with in a timely manner. In retaliation to their lack of prompt action, he removed all their freight and equipment from the station and dumped it on their "right of way" property. What this conflict was over and how it was resolved is not recorded, but what is known is that the merchandise was summarily returned to the warehouse and the station continued with business as usual. Old, stubborn Henry got his way.

The steady moving of freight in and out of the depot day after day provided an added benefit for the industrialist. It meant there was always a supply of grain, vegetables, fruit and "middlin" meat available in the store. Those who were present when the train station was torn down recalled seeing some plump rats, whose happy abode was consequently broken up. As was general practice in those days, produce and other staples were good barter at Johnson's store for wares carried in stock. A pound of butter was a monetary unit for a quantity of calico, coffee, sugar or other household utensils. Other standard fares included eggs, hides, tallow, beeswax, fruit and grain.

Henry Johnson, like other men of that time, took an active part in politics, debating the issues facing the country, as well as those of the local community. Such discussions usually took place in gatherings on the road and around the store's popular cracker barrel. During the Civil War, East Tennessee was divided between Union and Confederate sentiments, even though Tennessee had seceded from the Union. A portion of General Burnside's Union army passed through Johnson City during the latter part of the war and engaged a detachment of the enemy near Watauga, five miles east of the city, in what was known as "Carter's Depot." It is said that firing of the cannons could be heard all the way to Henry's Depot.

It was during the Civil War that one of the political campaigns raged in this section between Landon C. Haynes and P.C. Nelson for United States congressional representation. In this political battle, Johnson opposed Haynes.

In recognition of Haynes's influence and power, his supporters secured legislation and had the town renamed Haynesville. Those acquainted with Johnson remember that the surprise move seemed to have very little effect on him. The term Johnson's Depot had not, up to that time, been fraught with any particular desire to honor the founder of the city. The name was simply the logical and proper description of the train depot that Henry had built. After the change to Haynesville, the friends of Johnson, who would not remain silent on the issue, started a movement to have the old name restored. When the unassuming Johnson was questioned about it, he replied, in words that are very likely paraphrased: "I don't care a hang. They can call it Sally Ann if they want to."

At any rate, Henry's name was promptly restored after the Civil War, not back to Johnson's Depot, but to Johnson City, suggesting that the little village had finally grown up and become a city. Even before the Johnson v. Haynes hassle, the town citizens had addressed the designation of the settlement. A few believed it should carry the name of Tipton Jobe, whose home was in proximity to the center of the business district. Henry Johnson, as expected, had no problem with this label and even supported it. Tipton Jobe, a nephew of the original guarantor, Abraham Jobe, is said to have modestly declined the honor, allowing Johnson City to become the name. On December 1, 1869, Johnson City was granted a charter of incorporation; the city limits encompassed a half-mile radius from Johnson's Depot on Fountain Square. When the first city election was held on January 3, 1870, Henry Johnson was unanimously elected as its first mayor.

Henry Johnson died on February 25, 1874, at the age of sixty-four. The estimated population of the town then was 500. While it had been incorporated five years before his death, the charter was later abolished, and the section was made into one of the county taxing districts to be incorporated again about ten years later. The first corporate limits were again determined to be an imaginary circle with a radius of half a mile. The official population for 1880 was shown to be 654. At the time of Johnson's passing, several additional stores were operating in downtown Johnson City. The other buildings were first located mainly to the east, on what is now East Market Street, and then to the south, along Main Street between Fountain Square and Roan Street. At that time, until a decade later, two churches, some small shops and many vacant lots occupied the present principal block of the retail district.

Several individuals living in Johnson City at the time of Henry's death attended his funeral and recalled that it was as modest as the man to whom they were paying their last respects. The founder was buried in the Hoss family cemetery, considered far out of the city at that time and now near East Myrtle Avenue at the edge of Carnegie Addition. Mary followed her husband in death on November 2, 1888, and was buried beside him. Since the grave, as well as the cemetery, was not maintained properly over the years, eventually a movement was made to locate Henry's and Mary's remains to Oak Hill Cemetery, just a few blocks southwest of the spot on the railroad where the city was born. On March 26, 1874, the *Jonesborough Herald and Tribune* gave a lengthy obituary. It stated in part:

> *Eighteen years ago, Johnson located in Johnson City, where he has since remained a prominent and respected citizen. He was the first citizen of this place and to his influence, untiring energy and undaunted courage does Johnson City owe its origin, ascribing to him the honor so justly inherited of proudly bearing his name. The respect, universal regret, and sorrow manifested on his burial day, was unlike any that we have here witnessed previously and told plainly that he was beloved and respected by all who knew him.*

A DEBATING SOCIETY BECAME
SCIENCE HILL HIGH SCHOOL

S cience Hill High School has stood as the monumental fortress of education in Johnson City since 1860. An old high school annual bearing the title *The Argonaut* offers a brief historical glimpse of the cultural appetite in Johnson's Depot in 1860, when the population was estimated to be about five hundred residents. The Science Hill Debating Society organized that year in the Oak Grove community, located about two and a half miles north of the city limits in the Boones Creek area. Its membership included some dauntless minds of the day: J.M. Carr, H.H. Carr, William Taylor, I.E. Reeves, E.C. Reeves, F.A. Faw and John H. Bowman.

One year later, the organization relocated to the "School House" in Johnson's Depot that stood on Bush Creek Campground, currently located in the plot of land enclosed by four city streets—Watauga, Montgomery, Jackson and Winter. With the change in venue came new fervor, fresh energy and a stronger desire to excel and add zest and loyalty to the common cause. The society grew in number by annexing "the Town Boys" to the roll: J.M. Johnson, A.H. Yeager, E.F. Yeager, G.G. Yeager, Benjamin Akard, Elbert Akard and others. Just when the time seemed most favorable for the advancement of academic abilities in the village, the dreadful apparition of a civil war caused disorganization and disruption to so noble a beginning of prowess. The resulting call to arms depleted the ranks of the society for a few years.

In 1863, a new crude, hewn-log school building was built on Rome Hill, a short distance to the east along North Roan Street, within walking distance of Henry Johnson's train depot at Fountain Square and West Market Street. The rustic school functioned here for twenty-three years, until 1886, when the school moved down the hill to a spot near Brush Creek. A new building was constructed that served as a school during the week and a church on Sunday, promoting both education and religion. This school, like its predecessor, was built with hewn logs and consisted of one large room. Six steps led to the front door. Professor Lenoir served as principal and the sole teacher of the facility.

Unlike today's rigid grading system, the school judged students by their merit rather than pure subject knowledge. Students sat on long benches that were positioned against the wall. Desks were nothing more than rough wooden planks that sloped downward from the top. Courses included dictionary, Quackenbos's rhetoric, United States history, astronomy, Watts On Your Mind, Smith's grammar, arithmetic (boys only), Latin and writing. Instead of a school board determining the curriculum, the professor decided which subjects the pupils should take based on his assessment of each individual. Teachers were paid a salary from a Peabody Fund. Classes commenced promptly at 8:00 a.m. and dismissed at 4:00 p.m. Students had critical routine chores that had to be done immediately upon their arrival home from school. Although pupils began school at a very early age, they were forced to quit about the time they were eighteen years old.

Common events for these early schools were spelling bees, which gave students bragging rights if they could survive the fierce competition from others. Students and teachers immensely enjoyed these contests. During the course of a day, ample time was devoted for students to recite their lessons. No tests were given on the lesson material. Behavioral rules were strictly enforced, such as one that specified that girls and boys could not walk together while coming to or going from school. Many a young person tested that decree, only to end up on the end of the teacher's paddle.

In 1866, plans were afoot to build a "seminary building" at Johnson's Depot that everyone could attend to acquire a solid education. A prominent resident, Tipton Jobe, donated two and a half acres near the site of the old building for a new high school. The finished schoolhouse, said to be a "splendid structure," was dedicated to science. Since the new school sat majestically on Roam Hill, it soon was christened Science Hill Male and Female Institute (later renamed Science Hill High School and also referred to as Science Hill Academy).

The new facility was financed partially from private individuals and businesses and was a significant improvement over the previous schools. Instead of being constructed of wood, it was built from sturdy, hand-made bricks. It had two rooms downstairs and a large auditorium upstairs, which became a gathering place for a vast array of community events that included political rallies, theatre plays, meetings, lectures and business conferences. Wood stoves in all rooms knocked out the chill in frigid weather. Two student

A Debating Society Became Science Hill High School

The first brick Science Hill High School, built in 1867 on Roam Hill near Brush Creek. Local resident Tipton Jobe donated the two and a half acres of land. *Courtesy of Doris Cox Anderson (taken from 1939 Science Hill High School Annual,* The Wataugan).

responsibilities were to gather wood from around the hill and to fetch water from the Faw spring located at the corner of Roan and Market Streets. The ten-story John Sevier Hotel would later sit on the site where the popular spring was located.

With the new building came new aspirations and new ideals of modern thought. Expression and the spirit of debate were again aroused with the rapid increase of population in the village. The Debating Society once again flourished. New additions to the membership roll included some of the townsmen and citizens who occupied places of prominence: J.W. Crumley, A.F. Hoss, R.J. Rankin, J.C. King, W.W. Faw, S.S. Crumley, A.B. Bowman, Isaac Harr and Dr. J.W. Cox.

The Reverend J.B. Pence was chosen to be the first principal of the new school. The teachers were Mr. and Mrs. Evans, Mr. Barker, Mrs. Lusk, Mr. Templin, Miss Lelia Gentry and Miss Delia Buckley. In 1885, Mrs. John Templin (née Miss Sue McNeece) won the first scholarship offered at the school. It was said that the first student body of the school was so small that you could count its members on your fingers and toes. For several years, teachers were paid from a tuition fee of twelve dollars per term levied on students because the school received no city or state money. Sometimes the students were financially unable to pay their bills and gave the school promissory notes that the money would be paid after obtaining work. In 1884, the *Comet* painted a less than complimentary image of the school: "Science Hill is an eyesore to the town. It is rugged, ugly, uninviting, of no special blame on anyone, but it rests upon us all."

Within eight years, that scenario began to change when Johnson City took ownership of the educational institute and began paying teachers, thus making it a public high school. Since there were no assigned grades, students continued to study pretty much what they were assigned by their teachers. Between 1892 and 1902, the school saw accelerated growth rendering the building too small for the number of students attending. In 1902, a room was added downstairs and another one upstairs; both faced Roan Street. One was primarily for music instruction and resulted in the hiring of Miss Ida Baugh of Virginia as the school's first music teacher. Professor J.E. Crouch served as the new principal and tenth-grade teacher.

Additional grades began to be assigned, thus requiring the hiring of three additional teachers: Miss Moore, fifth grade; Miss Brown, sixth; and Professor Will Hatcher, ninth. The new school provided city water thereby eliminating frequent trips across the street to the Faw spring. Another significant change was the use of coal instead of wood for stoves. This building served the city's needs well for more than a quarter of a century, with such professors as Ramsey, Freeland, Easley, Powell, Johnson and others. However, time and an increasing city population brought the need for even larger facilities. This prompted the addition of a west wing in 1902.

During the 1909–10 Science Hill school year, enrollment grew to 144 students. By this time, Mr. Meadows was principal, but he served only one year and was replaced by Mr. Byrd. Two new teachers, Miss Willie Reeves (language) and Miss Elizabeth Carr (history) were added. The facility was again expanded to include four large rooms and a spacious study hall that also served as a classroom. Some of the students during this era who went on to prominence were Burr Harrison (photographer), Lee Harr (banker), Gunner Teilmann (florist) and Adam Bowman (judge).

Increasing student enrollment again caught up with Science Hill Academy. This time, remodeling was not the solution; a new, larger school building was desperately needed. The old structure was immediately destroyed. While the new school was being rebuilt adjacent to the old one, students were temporarily transferred to the Teacher's College, a state Normal School. The new facility brought with it a new heating system—central furnace heat replaced individual room heaters. By 1915, a full slate of twelve teachers and

A Debating Society Became Science Hill High School

The second brick Science Hill High School, built in 1910 adjacent to the old school.
Courtesy of Doris Cox Anderson (taken from 1939 Science Hill High School Annual, The Wataugan*).*

a senior class of fifty-two students were functioning under the principalship of Mr. T.E. Utterback.

Three years later, Mr. D.M. Andrews became superintendent of schools, and Mr. J.A. Tinsley served as principal. The school was still manned by twelve teachers: two English, two mathematics, one science, one Latin, one household arts, one art, one modern language, one commercial, one manual arts and one expression. Extracurricular activities at that time consisted of eight organizations or clubs, each meeting on Friday afternoons. Three literary societies were for boys and three were for girls. A Latin Club and a WMCA complemented them.

Two years later, the new, impressive high school looked pretty much the same; the hill had not yet been terraced, but eighty-eight steps had been put in place for reaching the school from Roan Street. Walking up them each morning gave students a cardiovascular workout before classes began. Miss

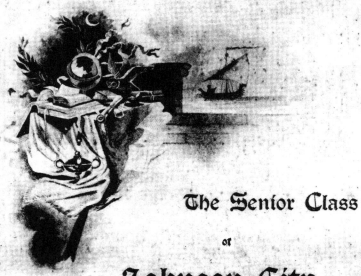

Class Motto:
Not Finished, but Begun

The Senior Class
of
Johnson City
High School

desires your presence at the

Commencement Exercises - - -

Friday Evening, May 18th
1894

A Science Hill High School Graduation program from Friday evening, August 18, 1894.
Courtesy of Doris Cox Anderson (taken from 1939 Science Hill High School Annual, The Wataugan*).*

A Debating Society Became Science Hill High School

Lucy Hatcher, a math teacher, became principal and served a long tenure in this position. D.R. Hayworth was appointed superintendent of schools. The subjects were the same as those included in the curriculum for 1918, except that the course expression was dropped.

When the class of 1925 graduated, Mr. C.E. Rogers replaced Hayworth as school superintendent. By then, the faculty had grown to twenty-four members, with seventy graduating students. The junior class had seventy-eight; the sophomore class, seventy-eight; and the freshman class, sixty-four. It was during this time that school officials included sports in the curriculum to broaden the Literary Society's 1860 vision of the future. Also, the year 1931 brought with it construction of the left (north) wing of the school that overlooked Water Street and an upgrade to modern equipment. The school's colors, which had previously been green and yellow, were changed to maroon and gold. Amusingly, this came about when the football team's jerseys became so worn that new ones were required. Not being able to obtain the old school colors, they were forced to choose a new color scheme.

Growth in the student body increased from just a handful of students in 1863 to 833 students in 1939. The senior class totaled 245 students. A threefold building program began in 1939 to provide for a gymnasium along the back (east) end of the property, an auditorium and additional classroom facilities. The faculty consisted of thirty-three regular teachers with college degrees, thirteen of them possessing master's degrees. For the next twenty-two years, few changes were made to the big brick building sitting on Rome (changed to Roan) Hill in downtown Johnson City.

In 1961, a new Science Hill High School was built along John Exum Parkway just north of the city. Although, consideration was given to changing the school name, most students wanted to retain the old designation for sentimental reasons. The school board agreed with their desire, although the new property contained no significant hills. The now empty downtown building was converted to South Junior High School and the original one was renamed North Junior High. The site that had been so prominent in providing for the educational needs of Johnson City was later razed to make space for a new public library; still later, it became the spot for expansion of the adjacent Munsey Memorial Methodist Church. The once noisy hill flaunting the merriment of scurrying schoolchildren became silenced forever.

Haskiel H. Dyer, a student, penned some beautifully expressed and fitting words about the old school in the 1915 school annual:

The historic evolution of Science Hill High School opens before us like a splendid vision. Touched by every impulse and stirred by every ambition to leave an impression upon the life of its devotee; its history has made its way into the annals of time. From its historic slope countless men and women have gone into the realm of active life, as the vapor drifts from the sea. From its height has been seen the past drift from the present to eternity. We watch yet the tide of humanity surge below from its better-fortified position than yesterday.

WERE THE TAYLOR BROTHERS FIDDLERS OR VIOLINISTS?

One of the most unusual political campaigns ever to transpire in the state of Tennessee was the now-famous 1886 governor's race, known as "the War of the Roses," between well-known local fiddle-playing brothers, Bob and Alf Taylor. The "Rose War" got its name from the civil wars fought over the throne of England from 1455 to 1487 between supporters of the House of Lancaster and those of the House of York. The badges they wore distinguished the two factions—one wore the red rose of Lancaster and the other the white rose of York. In the Tennessee version, the supporters of Bob, the Democratic challenger, wore the white rose of York on their lapels, while the followers of Alf, the Republican contender, donned the red rose of Lancaster. A person's preference of politics could be readily determined simply by noting the color of the rose on his or her lapel or buttonhole (although it was reported that some ladies forgot about politics and exchanged red and white roses in order to form bouquets for their favorite beaus).

Bob and Alf remained good-humored toward each other and well disciplined throughout the campaign, not allowing their differences in politics to thwart their relationship as siblings. Unlike most contests, in which candidates resort to mudslinging, the Taylor brothers spared one another and simultaneously entertained the crowds. It was the most unique campaign in Tennessee history. When the election was concluded, the white roses triumphed across the state, eventually bestowing upon Bob three terms as governor and one term as U.S. senator. Alf became governor for one stint in 1920.

Bob began traveling the lecture circuit with his very popular discourse, "The Fiddle and Bow," and Alf followed suit with the dissertation, "Yankee Doodle and Dixie." Was the elected official aligning himself as a fiddler or was he, in actuality, a violinist, applying the word in a more generic

Bob Taylor. *Courtesy of the 1921 book,* Old Limber or The Tale of The Taylors *by Delong Rice.*

Alf Taylor. *Courtesy of 1921 book,* Old Limber or The Tale of The Taylors *by Delong Rice.*

Were the Taylor Brothers Fiddlers or Violinists?

connotation? Satirist Ambrose Bierce once defined a fiddle as "an instrument designed to tickle human ears by friction of a horse's tail [the bow] on the entrails of a cat [the strings]." The violin/fiddle is one of the most intriguing instruments ever conceived, with a price tag ranging from an economical pawnshop model to a rare and priceless authentic Stradivarius. Not to be confused with the real thing was a "Stradivarius model," which was mass-produced in Germany during the early part of the twentieth century, selling for under fifteen dollars, including the case and bow.

Anyone who has mastered this unique contrivance will verify that it is a very difficult instrument to learn, requiring successful coordination of finger motions on the fretless (no ridges on the fingerboard like other instruments) strings with the difficult, fluctuating, syncopated long and short movements of the bow. Such a feat requires years to achieve proficiency. The most frequently asked question of any fiddler/violinist is: "What is the difference between a fiddle and a violin?" The answer is both simple and complex. If someone were to enter a music store and tell the attendant that he/she wanted to purchase one fiddle and one violin, the attendant would sell the customer two identical instruments. Such an action implies that the two devices are indistinguishable, rendering a fiddle a violin and a violin a fiddle. Some music scholars argue that the fiddle significantly predates the violin; in essence, making the latter a member of the fiddle family and suggesting that a violin is a fiddle but that a fiddle is not necessarily a violin.

If there are no physical differences between the two devices, except for some minor adjustments made to them after they are purchased, why are some musicians called fiddlers and others violinists? Obviously, the dissimilarity is more a function of the musician and the type of songs being played than the instrument itself. Perhaps the best way to distinguish between a fiddler and a violinist is to observe each one in action and note any differences firsthand.

Since most violinists play as a group member in an orchestra, they should be observed in a theatre setting. Such an ensemble finds the violinists clustered together onstage, their instruments against their chins, properly postured in chairs, attired in semiformal dress and interpreting notes from sheet music secured to music stands. The performers alternately maintain eye contact with their music and their conductor, the latter synchronizing all the musicians into one desired product. The audience, also properly dressed, sits motionless and appears to comprise people of above-average social class. Violin music is one of sheer beauty and power; the audience expresses its approval with thunderous applause at appropriate times. This genre adheres to a long-held strict written standard for holding the violin and bow and for playing from a script, leaving no room for improvising or straying. The violinists have specific "marching orders" on their music stands and are fully committed to them, along with their conductor's leadership. The selections consist mostly of operatic and classical music from the masters—sonatas, suites and concertos. The musicians demonstrate a full understanding of each selection that includes the time period and the composer's intent for the piece.

Fiddlers are of a different breed. They typically play in an old-time, bluegrass, Cajun, western swing or country gathering. A trip to one of their gigs is a vastly dissimilar experience from what a violinist would provide. In an old-time string band, the fiddler places the instrument against the shoulder, taking the lead as if he or she were the conductor, standing as opposed to sitting and dressed in casual garb. A fiddler does not use a music stand, but instead, plays by ear, the notes mysteriously evolving from the head through the heart and into the strings. Fiddle music is not so much one of beauty, but of rhythmic energy, haunting and melodious, soaring heavenward, full of life. The audiences are equally casually dressed and express their approval not with thunderous applause, but by clapping to the beat, perhaps singing along, tapping their toes and dancing. The fiddler appears to be in a daze, with a glazed look in his/her eyes, playing effortlessly and incessantly with little sign of fatigue, stringing melodic notes together like a skilled knitter and rarely playing a tune the same way twice. The performer takes a lifeless skeletal song structure and imparts life into it with his/her fiddle. A fiddler's repertoire consists mainly of ballads, hoedowns, jigs, reels, waltzes, blues, flings and hornpipes. Like favorite jokes, the tunes have been circulated over the centuries from player to player, who acquire them, perhaps make minor changes and pass them on to others—a tradition unheard of in the violinists' camp.

Many well-rounded musicians can comfortably play the violin or fiddle one moment and magically transform it into the other the next. The Irish folklorist, Breandan Breathnach, once stated, "A violinist is not an educated fiddler any more than a fiddler is an untutored violinist." *Fiddler Magazine* humorously defines a fiddle as "a violin with attitude." Scores of jokes exist that contrast fiddlers with violinists; some are rather unflattering. Some fiddler yarns include: Calling a fiddler a violinist is a supreme insult; labeling a violinist a fiddler is the ultimate compliment. The encore for a fiddler is "more, more, more"; requests for a violinist are "less, less, less."

Jokes from the other camp would suggest a different scenario: Violinists put strings on their instruments not "strangs." A surefire way to drive someone totally insane is to nail his/her shoes to the floor and play a fast-moving fiddle tune. And then there is this comical ditty: "A young theologian named

Were the Taylor Brothers Fiddlers or Violinists?

Fiddle refused to accept an honorary doctor of divinity degree declaring, 'It's one thing to be Fiddle, yet another to be Fiddle DD.'"

Returning to the question of whether Bob Taylor was a fiddler or a violinist, perhaps it is best to let the noted politician settle the issue himself in an excerpt from a speech dated April 24, 1889, addressed to "My Dear Fellow Sawyers [referring to someone who 'saws' on the old fiddle]":

> *I still have fond recollections of every fiddler who played at the old-time country-dance, and when I hear those sweet old tunes, even now it is difficult for me to keep my soul above my socks...The classics of Mozart and Mendelssohn are grand and glorious to me, but I cannot be persuaded to turn my back on the classics of plain country fiddlers.*

JOHNSON CITY'S
LOVE AFFAIR WITH THE
COUNTY FAIR

Johnson City has had a longstanding love affair with county fairs, extending back to 1897, when the first tri-county fair rolled into the quaint township of about forty-five hundred inhabitants. The intimate relationship continues to this day.

The Thursday, October 3, 1901 edition of the *Comet* newspaper posted an attention-grabbing headline on its front page: "Tri-County Fair—Johnson City, Tennessee—Oct. 8, 9, 10, 11, 1901." It displayed a list of thirty-eight competitions to be held during the four-day event, one of the most unusual of which was the Fairbank's Glycerine Tar Soap Shampooing Contest. Male contestants were supplied with a tin basin of warm water and a three-ounce sample of the soap product. They were told to remove their coats, roll up their sleeves, place a towel around their necks and, at a signal from the board of judges, begin making a lather and simultaneously apply it to the scalp and hair. The person who accumulated the most lather on his head at the end of five minutes was awarded one hundred cakes of Fairbank's Glycerine Tar Soap.

The paper next offered a sampling of additional contests, sponsors and prizes awarded:

> *Best homemade chocolate candy: Seibert, Whitman and Company; one pair ladies fine shoes valued at $8.00.*
> *Prettiest baby under two years of age: Enterprise Shoe Company; one pair of the finest shoes made.*
> *Best half bushel of turnips: J.S. Byrd & Company; one cranberry axe.*
> *Best half bushel of sweet potatoes: Gump Brothers, Clothiers; one man's fine hat.*

Tri-County
F*AIR****
Johnson City, Tenn.,
Oct. 8, 9, 10, 11, 1901.

A Tri-County Fair newspaper ad from the *Comet*, dated October 3, 1901. *Courtesy of the Microfilm Library, East Tennessee State University.*

A Fairbank's Glycerine Tar Soap advertisement from 1902. *Courtesy of the Bob Cox Collection.*

Prettiest and healthiest baby under one year of age raised on Horlick's Malted Milk: Horlick's Food Company; four bottles of malted milk.
Best loaf of bread baked on a Blue Flame Oil Stove: Summers, Barton & Parrott; one nickel plated coffee pot.
Best cocoanut cream cake made with Dunham's Shred Coconut: M.I. Gump Grocery; twelve packages of the product.

An Appalachian District Fair newspaper ad from the *Johnson City Staff-News*, dated October 17, 1928. *Courtesy of the Microfilm Library, East Tennessee State University.*

Best display of drawn thread work: Ziegler Brothers Shoes; one pair of ladies shoes valued at $3.50.

Longest handled gourd: City Drug Store; one-pound of Bull Durham Tobacco.

Best pair of homemade horseshoes: G.C. Dromgoole; one pound of grape tobacco.

Best homemade broom: G.C. Dromgoole; one pound of grape tobacco.

On Tuesday, October 16, 1928, the perennial fair acquired a new name, the Appalachian District Fair, when it began a five-day run at Keystone Field. It discreetly came into existence two years prior, known as the Gray Station Fair, operating out of the old Gray Station School as a half-day event. In 1931, the traveling show returned to Gray, where it remains to this day.

The 1928 premier extravaganza was later reported in the *Johnson City Staff-News* as the most complete and elaborate fair ever staged at any district event of its kind. The newspaper provided a day-by-day account of the festivities. They got underway at 9:00 a.m., with a parade of animals, performers and workers traveling east from Fountain Square on Main Street to the fairgrounds. Hordes of excited people lined the streets of the parade route. Gates officially opened at 9:30 that morning, followed by an unusual daylight fireworks display, signaling to townspeople that the fair was open for business. Admission was twenty-five cents for children and fifty cents for adults. The exposition ran from Tuesday, October 16, to Saturday, October 20, with each day highlighting a different theme: Tuesday was "Home Coming Day"; Wednesday, "Tennessee Day"; Thursday, "Virginia and Carolina Day"; Friday, "School Day"; and Saturday, "Mardi Gras Day." The promoters were clearly attempting to boost attendance and revenues by attracting people from neighboring counties and states.

The vaudeville and circus acts, alleged to be "highly entertaining, amusing and educational," were presented to cheering crowds daily in front of a large grandstand, where specialized equipment had been erected for the performers. The entertainment numbers were alleged to be "the most complete and elaborate ever staged at any district fair." The performances, according to hundreds of attending visitors, ranked among those presented at many of the larger, highly publicized state fairs.

An array of talent was paraded before the grandstands during the five-day event. Swan Ringen's Diving Girls proved to be one of the biggest sensations of the afternoon's entertainment. The star's plunge into a six-foot tank of water from a platform towering seventy-five feet off the ground was acclaimed by many to be one of the best features of the week. She received tremendous applause at the conclusion of her perilous feat. The four other diving girls, described as "bathing beauties," were likewise well received by the crowd.

Another act, the Five Fearless Fliers, comprising two men and three women, was reported to be "one of the greatest and most sensational high trapeze and casting displays ever presented in the area." Swinging to and fro from their lofty rigging, these intrepid artists fearlessly tossed one another back and forth, somersaulting into the hands of their respective assistants. The act culminated with one artist, blindfolded and tied in a sack, making a triple somersault through the air and being caught by an associate. The skill and ease with which the gymnasts performed their amazing numbers took the audience by storm, and they showed their approval with repeated thundering ovations.

Next, the Merrell brothers and sisters, advertised as "equilibrists, trapeze and slack wire performers," came to Johnson City directly from the Mississippi State Fair. They, too, were a breathtaking hit, receiving a similar enthusiastic response during their performance.

The Armstrong Company, featuring coterie bar work, as well as solo trick wire acts, was both compelling and amusing to its audiences. One stunt was the appearance of "Krazy Kar," a trick Ford that did everything but stand on its radiator cap.

The J.J. Page Exposition Shows, a Johnson City, winter-based carnival that was in its infancy in 1928, provided entertaining sideshows and thrilling rides. The newspaper commented that the Page Carnival was "of a high standard and many new, entertaining, amusing and education features have been added to the show since it last appeared in Johnson City." The Page Carnival would have sustaining success and remain in operation until the early 1950s.

On Tuesday, an open-air band concert began at 1:30 p.m., but rain forced its relocation to the Industrial Exhibit tent. The massive crowd listened attentively

GRAY'S STATION

FAIR

ADMIT ONE

An admission ticket used on August 3, 1935, to attend the Gray's Station Fair, which made an annual visit to the community. *Courtesy of the Bob Cox Collection.*

and loudly applauded the numbers rendered. Inclement weather also forced the cancellation of a fireworks display that was planned for that evening. However, the nocturnal light show was presented on subsequent nights without a hitch. Tuesday's special event was a horseshoe-pitching contest.

Exhibits of flowers and garden products were judged Tuesday, with first- and second-place prizes awarded. Floriculture items included zinnias, dahlias, basket mixed flowers, dozens of roses, basket marigolds and different varieties of cut flowers. Potted plants were fern, begonia, hanging basket, geranium, sultana and centerpiece. Garden products consisted of an assortment of fifteen fresh vegetables, tomatoes, fifteen garden seeds, oyster plant, Swiss chard, gallon peanuts and kohlrabi.

On Wednesday night, wet weather prevented the presentation of several acts; damp rigging made it too dangerous for performers to attempt certain feats, but the missed performances were added to the Saturday schedule. Horseshoe-pitching finals were held on the second day.

Thursday offered a cow-calling contest, with the winner appropriately awarded a silver cowbell. Also on that day was a horse-riding promenade. The third day witnessed another day of judging in the agricultural and livestock classes, where the judges found a surprising number and variety of exhibits. Judging and awarding prizes continued daily until the close of the fair.

At a meeting of the city commission on Thursday afternoon, a resolution was adopted at city hall endorsing the proclamation of Mayor W.J. Barton that called for the closing of municipal business Friday to allow employees to attend the much-talked-about fair. The order was immediately carried out, and all city offices were ordered to close that day, which was officially declared "Johnson City Day." The city commission, by its action, strongly urged area businesses to do the same thing. A special program was arranged for Friday to celebrate the city's newly proclaimed holiday. Friday was designated as "School Day," with area schools competing in a field meet; all the while, the many features of the fair continued running at full pace.

Saturday's "Mardi Gras Day" signaled the finale of the first-ever district fair, but not before a unique overhead firework spectacular, featuring, in lights, the destruction of a Spanish village, an idea conceived by Jean Dagar of the Ellwood Dillin organization in Johnson City. The company was responsible for all the fair's exhibits, equipment and concessions. The final curtain came down with a "red-fire" parade, many auction sales of surplus exhibits and merchandise on display on the grounds.

Today, the Appalachian District Fair, although appreciably different from its ancestors of days past, remains a tireless staple of entertainment for residents and visitors alike.

BUSINESSES FLOURISHED
AT THE TURN OF THE CENTURY

Vintage city directories serve as a great source of information for historians, providing detailed information about the city at that particular time in history, including classified businesses, a listing of streets and residents and an alphabetized record of the populace.

One Johnson City directory for 1911 is a manifestation of the era, with such business categories as banks; barbers; blacksmiths and wheelwrights; boardinghouses; buggies and wagons; carriage and wagon dealers; cigars and tobacco; coffins and caskets; embalmers, founders and machinists; gun- and locksmiths; harness and saddlery; horseshoe services; livery, feed and sale stables; mills (saw and planing); newspapers and periodicals; queensware; railroads; sewing machines; shoemakers; street railway companies; and undertakers.

An index of advertisements revealed thirty-seven businesses, including: America Lumber Co., Ambrust-Smith Co. (furniture), I.N. Beckner (jeweler), Brading and Marshall (lumber supplies), the *Comet* (newspaper), Johnson City Bottling Works (Hires' Root Beer and Ko-Conola), R.C. Hunter (insurance) and Summers-Parrott Co. (hardware).

Johnson City has had a long love affair with these old directories; the first one was produced in 1909, when the population was about nine thousand. A walk through the directory offers a unique peek into the workings of the city at a time when its streets were just being paved and horses and carriages were its standard mode of transportation. This was also the age of trolleys, with parallel metal tracks running down the center of some of the main streets and overhead electrical cables that powered the cars.

The *1909 Street Guide* was a bit primitive compared to later editions. The 121-page book listed sixty city streets and avenues, with 24 pages identifying the people living on the streets. The roads were Afton, Ash, Baxter, Boone,

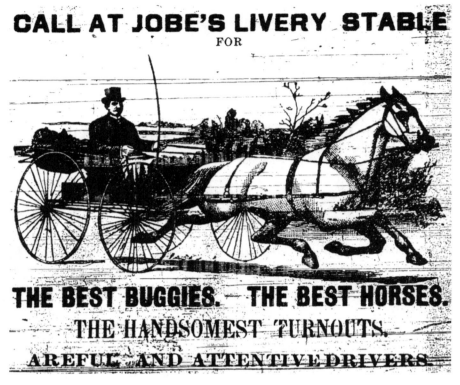

An advertisement for Jobe's Livery Stable on West Main Street, from the *Comet*, May 30, 1889. *Courtesy of the Microfilm Library, East Tennessee State University.*

Buffalo, Carnegie, Cherokee Road, Cherry, Chestnut, Commerce, Division, Eighth, Elm, Elmo, Ernest, Fairview, Fifth, Fourth, Fulton, Grover, Hamilton, Harris, Henry, Holston, Humboldt, Ivy, Jobe, King, Lamont, Locust, Main, Maple, Market, Maupin, Millard, Montgomery, Myrtle, New, Ninth, Oak, Pine, Popular, Public Square, Railroad, Roan, Second, Seventh, Sixth, Spring, Stuart, Summer, Tenth, Third, Unaka, Walnut, Watauga, Wellborn, Whitney, Willow and Winter.

Other sources of nearly forgotten history are vintage newspapers. A 1903 clipping from the *Comet* gave honorable mention to several downtown business establishments that were said to be rock-solid contributors to the city's fast-paced growth:

The Unaka National Bank at Main and Public Square was reported to be one of the strongest financial institutions in Northeast Tennessee, growing stronger with each passing year, both in sales revenues and in public esteem. It was the result of a state bank organized in Johnson City in 1896 by the

Businesses Flourished at the Turn of the Century

late John D. Cox of Jonesboro and his associates. The bank's beginning was a modest one, but its success was ensured from the outset by the character and financial standing of its promoters. While yet a state bank, the capital was increased to $37,500 to meet the demands of the business. In 1901, a national banking charter was taken out and the name of Unaka National Bank was adopted. Correspondingly, the capital was increased to $50,000. The aim of management was obvious by the building up of a surplus. Within two years, an excess fund of $10,000 grew even larger with time. The bank maintained the steadfast confidence of the public and its patrons because of the body of officials who gave it their best efforts. One of the most popular and efficient bankers in the section, Tate L. Earnest, was cashier, and Adam Crouch served as assistant cashier. The list of stockholders comprised some of Washington County's wealthiest men, who became a source of strength to the institution. Deposit figures, taken from the official public bank reports, were listed for the seven-year period between 1897 and 1903:

1897: $22,105
1898: $51,346
1899: $72,936
1900: $113,430
1901: $140,103
1902: $145,835
1903: $191,837.

Although all mercantile, wholesale and industrial houses in Johnson City were doing a brisk business during these prosperous times, M.I. Gump Wholesale Grocery, located at Roan and Southern Railway Station, was the recognized leader of the wholesale grocery business. An examination of the store's books showed a steady annual increase in sales since the establishment of the business in 1898. All goods handled by Mr. Gump were said to be of the highest quality and were sold precisely as advertised. Large consignments were daily sent from Gump's wholesale business to all parts of the state and North Carolina. Mr. Gump was a native of Johnson City and employed three local employees in various capacities in the store.

Miss Hardy, Millinery at 237 East Main was reported to be one of the most attractive stores, beautifying Main Street with its elegant millinery emporium of the owner, Johnson City's fashionable milliner. Within a two-year period, the storeowner achieved a thriving business brought about by her fine taste and popularity amongst her many customers. Miss Hardy's parlors were always well stocked with seasonable hats of all types. She carried a line of chapeaux (headdress with a shaped crown and usually a bonnet that protected the head from inclement weather) and bonnets of eye-catching design. She also displayed a sizable stock of ribbons, silks flowers, veils and dainty accessories to the feminine toilet. Her trade was patronized from the most select circles of Johnson City and surrounding area. She was known to always extend a cheerful welcome to all who visited her store.

Another business, City Stables, located at 125 West Market, was owned by W.T. Givens and managed by W.C. Snapp. It was the easy winner in Johnson City liveries for top-quality care, feeding and stabling of horses for pay. Mr. Givens was a transplanted Kentuckian with the essential ability to accurately judge horseflesh, and he would have nothing but sound, swift, young roadsters in his stables. Since opening his trade in 1900, he established a large patronage, owing chiefly to the fact that his turnouts were serviceable, comfortable and handsome. His stables measured 135 by 90 feet and accommodated one hundred horses. Mr. Givens also owned a feed stable, which was largely patronized by townspeople.

In an era of horse and buggy, Will I. Hart & Company at 101 East Market was in great demand for its services. The businessman, well experienced in the harness business, manufactured hand-made harnesses, saddles, bridles, collars, whips, leggings and an assortment of horse millinery. Since its inception in 1894, trade increased tremendously in all parts of the city and surrounding county. The firm employed four experienced men, who received ample wages in return for their services. Mr. Hart had resided in Johnson City for the past twenty-five years and did an extensive business. He acquired a large acquaintance and was held in high esteem by the populace.

Another longtime operation was Johnson City Foundry and Machine Works, situated at the corner of Cherry and Ernest Streets. Organized in 1884, this business had the distinction of being the second earliest established industry in town. The enterprise manufactured woodworking machinery, water wheels, brass and iron castings and forgings. It also engaged in major repair work. The foundry benefited from an abundance of raw material within easy access and an unlimited fuel supply in proximity to Johnson City. The firm was among the first manufacturers to realize this opportunity and take advantage of this fact. The massive plant covered over two acres of land. Seventy-five men were employed, with a payroll of $550 per week—at that time, a significant income. Within a relatively short time, the foundry received large contracts from every part of the country.

Another business that was significant at the time was T.J. Galloway's Johnson City Corn Mills at 205 Spring Street. The entrepreneur established a wholesale grain, feed and corn mills business in 1900. It immediately

Johnson City Foundry and Machine Works

All Kinds of Repair Work.   Johnson City, Tenn.

MANUFACTURERS OF

Log and Lumber Cars, Saw Mill Machinery, Tram Cars and Trucks.

GENERAL MACHINE SHOP REPAIRS

Johnson City Cemetery, Whitney nr Main, James Mumpire keeper

The Comet | Progressive

CY H. LYLE, Editor and Owner | Democratic

Summers-Parrott Hardware Co.

STOVES, VEHICLES, PAINTS. Railroad, Mill and Builders' Supplies

JOHNSON CITY BOTTLING WORKS

Phone 25

Bottlers of HIRES' ROOT BEER and KO-CONOLA

The WATAUGA EUROPEAN

Only Up-to-Date Place in City.   Oysters, Fish and Game in Season.

A collage of six advertisements of successful businesses, from the 1909 Piedmont City Directory. *Courtesy of the Archives of Appalachia, East Tennessee State University.*

proved to be a valuable addition to the commercial and industrial resources of the city. The company remained in almost constant operation, producing a wide variety of nutritious feed and cornmeal of the highest grade to be found. An advertisement from that era claimed that all products were of the purest quality and urged patrons to call phone number 138 if they had any questions.

Another city superstar was S.B. White at 111 Spring Street. A news clipping commented that the successful financial climate was bringing in a considerable amount of income for merchants. It singled out S.B. White as a forerunner, producing stoves and tin wares, furnaces, a complete line of china, queensware and lamps. General repair work was also done in spouting and guttering. It also did furnace work on a large scale. Fancy china was sold all over the city, region and county. Mr. White's business increased 30 percent in six months since the beginning of 1903. The *Comet* recommended this store as being first class in every respect.

These early businesses and others remained in operation for many years, making their marks on Henry Johnson's rapidly growing town and contributing to its mammoth success.

EVOLUTION OF
JOHNSON'S DEPOT INTO A
MULTI-RAILROAD TOWN

The manifestation of several railroads in the early days of Johnson City was an innate extension of its natural location, situated at the crossroads of mountain country. A document from that period stated that, by locating a plot of high ground in the city and observing the land contours firsthand, one could readily authenticate this fact. This pristine region was once referred to as "where springtime spends the summer."

The city was ideally at the convergence of travel between east and west, north and south and past and present. The region eventually developed from one of an almost primitive means of transportation to one with numerous railroads that necessitated a great deal of time, labor and money to accomplish. The emergence of the big engines occurred at a time when beasts of burden, sledges and wagons were still being employed as the only means of travel over the many remote, mountainous trails in the isolated mountain districts of East Tennessee and Western North Carolina. The coming of rail systems provided a stark contrast in the area as the city began a slow transition from primitive oxcarts to futuristic aircraft.

With time, a network of highways covered the Southern Mountain Region. To the south, highways and trails stretched like multiple ribbons toward Florida. A glance westward revealed many trunk lines over which a multitude of travelers journeyed each year. These trekkers soon had numbers of highways to choose from that led north from this section. The highways were described as being well constructed, easy to follow and relatively safe, considering the curves and steep grades with which the builders had to contend. This vast highway network allowed modern busses and trailer trucks to carry loads across the mountains, something heretofore not possible. Many tourists became attracted to this section because Johnson City was starting to be advertised as "the Switzerland of America."

The Southern Railway depot, situated between North Roan and West Market Streets along Brush Creek. *Courtesy of the Archives of Appalachia, East Tennessee State University.*

Within a relatively short time, Johnson City could boast five railway facilities operating within its ever-expanding town limits: Southern Railway, (originally known as the East Tennessee, Virginia and Georgia Railroad); East Tennessee and Western North Carolina (ET&WNC); Carolina, Clinchfield and Ohio Railroad (CC&O); Virginia and Southwestern; and the Johnson City Southern (Embreeville extension of the Southern).

The first rail system that became a regular in Johnson City was the East Tennessee, Virginia and Georgia Railroad, which later shortened its name to the Southern Railway. It originated in 1848 as the East Tennessee and Virginia Railroad. Located on its New York–Washington–Memphis short line route, the rail system passed through Johnson City, connecting the South and West with the North and East. This railroad gave Johnson City four local passenger stops and four limited ones, and it was said to haul the finest equipment and provide excellent service. The Embreeville Branch of the Southern Railway afforded supplementary service to and from Johnson City. Its existence became warranted because one of the largest zinc deposits in the United States was located there. Johnson City's ideal spot at the crossing of the Carolina, Clinchfield and Ohio Railroad and the Southern Railroad furnished the city trunk with line service in all directions. In its heyday, the city maintained a hefty operating schedule of eighteen passenger trains arriving and departing daily.

The Southern Railway was responsible for one of the most legendary train songs, "Wreck of the Old 97," ever recorded in American history. On September 27, 1903, Engine 1102, a mail train, was traveling from

Evolution of Johnson's Depot into a Multi-Railroad Town

The East Tennessee and Western North Carolina Railroad depot that was located on Buffalo Street. *Courtesy of the Archives of Appalachia, East Tennessee State University.*

Monroe, Virginia, to Spencer, North Carolina, when it derailed and tumbled seventy-five feet from Stillhouse Trestle near Danville, Virginia. Nine of its sixteen crew members perished in the mishap. The train's always-on-time reputation likely resulted in its traveling at excessive speeds to make up for lost time, which possibly contributed to the accident. The train was known to dangerously attain speeds in excess of sixty miles an hour, even on the most treacherous curves of the mountain track. "Old 97" was just one of many "tragedy" songs written during that colorful era. Virginia songster Henry Whitter originally recorded the "Wreck" for Okeh Records, but it was balladeer Vernon Dalhart who turned the song into the first million-selling hit in the United States. Since that time, country artists Johnny Cash, Boxcar Willie, Flatt and Scruggs, Hank Snow and countless others have further popularized the song and kept the memory of the awful derailment alive.

Another significant rail venture was the East Tennessee and Western North Carolina Railroad (ET&WNC, affectionately known as "Tweetsie") that operated between Johnson City and Boone, North Carolina, penetrating the very heart of the mountainous region. It began in 1866 and became the first train to cross the Blue Ridge Mountains. Some folks contended that before Tweetsie came into existence, the only way to get to Boone was to be born there. The train's daily run was in proximity to Cranberry, North Carolina, where some of the finest magnetic iron ore in America was located. The railroad's unique nickname was chosen by nearby mountaineers, who possessed a warm spot in their hearts for the beloved little narrow-gauge train. In addition to its normal daily business runs, the company occasionally offered affordable weekend sightseeing excursions during peak seasons to permit tourists to enjoy some of the most stunning scenery in America.

The Tweetsie Railroad, whose general offices and terminal were in Johnson City, also penetrated one of the richest mineral and timber sections of the Blue Ridge Mountains in Western North Carolina. Consequently, many summer resorts began to spring up, attracting tourists from all parts of the country. Passengers were engrossed by the beautiful and picturesque sights visible from the train as it passed through deep gorges, swayed around perpendicular cliffs and climbed high mountain ridges. The journey was breathtaking. Declining economic conditions and other factors began to signal the end of the Tweetsie. It made its final business voyage in 1950, but it was brought back to life in 1956 to offer sightseeing trips along a three-mile section of track at Blowing Rock, North Carolina.

In 1886, the need for another railroad line emerged primarily due to the need to transport iron ore from nearby North Carolina to Ashland and Ironton, Kentucky. Two production businesses that required twenty-six trainloads of the metal daily had been receiving it from states west of the Mississippi River. Local industrialists envisioned an opportunity for profit, but the venture would be a caveat—a new and expensive railroad would have to be built. Johnson City industrialist and former Union Civil War General John T. Wilder organized an aggregation of investors on September 30, 1887, and began selling bonds. Johnson City donated $75,000 to the venture, which was to be called the Carolina, Cincinnati and Chicago Railroad, nicknamed the "3Cs" Railroad.

Expectations were high, especially after an 1890 brochure proclaimed Johnson City as "The Future Iron and Steel Manufacturing Center of the South—The Only Town in the South Where Bessemer Pig Can be Manufactured for Only $10 Per Ton." The exciting news brought with it, almost overnight, increased demand for real estate and new industries. A horde of opportunity-seeking newcomers arrived in Johnson City in search of a way to cash in on the boom. With these visitors came such needs as additional housing, stores, banks, office buildings, brick manufacturers, planing mills, sawmills, lumber companies, a cigar box factory, a cannery and a soap factory. While surveying for the new railroad, a leading engineer from that era commented that if there were no other considerations, the vast quantity and variety of timber alone would justify the lucrative venture.

Regrettably, just when everything looked optimistic, the 3Cs Railroad faulted on its bonds and summarily declared bankruptcy. The reason for the debacle was that new deposits of iron ore were discovered in other states,

Evolution of Johnson's Depot into a Multi-Railroad Town

The Carolina, Clinchfield and Ohio Railway (CC&O) depot on Boone Street. *Courtesy of the Archives of Appalachia, East Tennessee State University.*

thereby reducing the demand for Cranberry ore. As quickly as the boom appeared, it abruptly dissipated, halting the railroad venture literally in its tracks after a small section of it was laid. Fortunately and surprisingly, the city was spared its $75,000 loss when a court ruled that, since the railroad was never completed, the city did not owe the money.

Another rail system, the Carolina, Clinchfield and Ohio Railroad (CC&O), became a major contributor to East Tennessee's history, with four passenger trains running daily. The rail system began with high expectations as a transportation and commercial route from the Ohio Valley to Charleston, South Carolina, but the Appalachian mountain barrier made its completion a formidable task. The company's origins can be traced to 1894, when the Ohio River and Charleston Railway Company began operation. Southwest Virginia native, George L. Carter, acquired the CC&O in 1902 and gave it a new name, the South and Western Railroad, offering stiff competition to the Southern. Under Carter's able guidance, the railroad grew rapidly until 1905, when John B. Dennis and his associates took over its operation and renamed it the Clinchfield Railroad. In 1908, the company became the Carolina, Clinchfield and Ohio Railway, with track stretching from the coal-mining region surrounding Dante, Virginia, on the north to Spartanburg, South Carolina, on the south.

The CC&O's enormous engines and lengthy trains were directly opposite those of ET&WNC's narrow-gauge rail system. The train's headquarters were in Erwin, with a depot in Johnson City. Over this line, which led to the coalfields of Virginia and Kentucky, passed the fastest freight train of its kind in the world. The company provided the shortest route from Cincinnati to all South and Southeastern coastal points and the Panama Canal. The connection with the Chesapeake and Ohio Railroad caused the investiture of passenger and freight service that was said to be unexcelled. The line proved a time saver for north- and south-bound passengers and freight deliveries. The CC&O passed through a historical and picturesque section of the very heart of the Blue Ridge Mountains, over what was termed by many construction engineers as "a marvelous piece of railroad engineering." Tunnels were numerous and much improved over previous ones, eliminating unpleasant conditions such as annoying odors. The completion of this route in 1911 gave Johnson City what was badly needed—competitive freight rates and direct service to the Northwest and Southeast.

Looking back on this country's golden age of railroading, there can be no doubt that the many railroads that chugged, huffed, puffed, wailed and blocked traffic as they maneuvered through the city each day for many years played a momentous role in Johnson City becoming what it is today.

THE NEW "SOLDIERS' HOME"
WAS A MOMENTOUS EVENT

January 28, 1901, was a momentous day in the annals of Johnson City history. On that date, Congress approved the city as a recipient of the Mountain Branch of the National Home for Disabled Volunteer Soldiers.

Two undated, but believed to be from about 1901, newspaper articles from the *Comet* offer some interesting information on the selection of property for the new facility. After approval of the government site, a sticky issue had to be quickly resolved—specifically, where to locate the imposing new complex. As with most matters of this nature, there were varying opinions as to where the home should be built, driven primarily by economic considerations. The topic was pondered and debated, causing the matter to be unresolved for a period of time. One newspaper headline from that era stated: "The Soldiers' Home Will Undoubtedly Be Located On the Lyle Property." The clipping noted that the site, selected by the board of managers, was two miles southwest of the city and embraced what was known primarily as the Lyle property, lying along the north side of the Southern railroad tracks.

The announcement stunned many residents because this property had not previously been under active consideration. Reportedly, the selection committee was traveling by train from Johnson City to Jonesboro and passed by the Lyle land. Impressed by the surrounding beautiful scenery of nearby Buffalo Mountain, the group requested a walking tour of the area. After inspecting the terrain, the group assembled in a detached railcar and surprisingly made a hasty decision to acquire it. This occurred just prior to the men being picked up by a vestibule train, a vehicle specially modified with a covering between adjoining cars that allowed passengers to traverse the train's entire length without being exposed to the elements. Their pick for the site was contingent upon the property having a sufficient water supply and a satisfactory sewerage system. Acquisition of the 445 acres of

A 1914 postcard shows the view of the Soldiers' Home bandstand and beautiful Buffalo Mountain in the background. *Courtesy of the Bob Cox Collection.*

land averaged fifty dollars per acre. The six landowners (and acreage) were C.J. Lyle (120), John F. Lyle (119), W.P. Miller (69), Robert F. Hale (61), J.M. Martin (43) and Joseph P. Lyle (33).

The new military reservation was to be located on a plateau running parallel to the Southern Railroad tracks, near the head of Brush Creek. The paper stated that from a point on this plateau, a person could view almost every mile of the Southern Railway route down to Watauga Station. As exciting as the selection was to many people, it lacked unanimity; some citizens were not happy with the choice. As expected, General John T. Wilder, a Johnson City resident for ten years, made it known that he opposed the site, saying that he thought the Carnegie location on the east side of town was a much better option. Wilder, the developer of the Carnegie Hotel and adjoining property in Johnson City, avowed that it would have been a more impressive setting because it was located on high ground overlooking the city and commanded a marvelous view of the valley and a long stretch of land belonging to the Southern Railway. The former Civil War general further argued that Piney Ridge was a mile away from Carnegie and that to the south was picturesque Buffalo Mountain. He evoked the "mind's eye" by declaring, in pictographic language:

The city sleeps in the gap, but the most beautiful part of it all is the great Unaka Mountain piled up in the hazy distance like the great waves of a beautiful sea. The towering peaks of the Mitchell, Roan and Grandfather mountains lifting their blue beards into the sky make an inspiring scene that rests the eye and refreshes the mind. When the sun went down in the west and there are no clouds to intervene, the Cloudland Hotel, located at top to Roan Mountain twenty-five miles away and over 6,000 feet high, was visible to the naked eye.

The New "Soldiers' Home" Was a Momentous Event

Soldiers' Home Memorial Hall Opera House was a favorite leisure spot, where soldiers and local residents regularly received a heavy dose of quality entertainment. *Courtesy of the Bob Cox Collection.*

Wilder declared that the Carnegie property had an inspiring view that had the appearance of some ancient castle or fortification. All this, he claimed, was lost at the Lyle setting because Buffalo Mountain, as beautiful as it was, blocked the view of the greater mountain ranges beyond. Wilder concluded his comments in a most gracious and humble manner:

> *Locally, the Lyle place, which is west of Johnson City and near the railroad, is a beautiful place for the home; the great thing lacking is the meager sweep of the vision. But either one of the places is the most beautiful that could be found in East Tennessee.*

With that thorny issue of property selection behind them, city officials began preparations to build on the newly acquired site. The construction cost exceeded $2 million, a huge sum of money at the turn of the century. In just over ten years, Soldiers' Home administered quality care for an average of fifteen hundred soldiers year-round and employed about five hundred workers. Much forethought went into the architectural design of the sprawling buildings. The home, after completion, was believed to be the finest aggregation of beautifully designed buildings of its kind anywhere in the world.

The grounds comprised more than 450 acres, with 200 acres allotted for farming, 50 acres of prime forest set aside for a zoological park consisting of elk, bear and other wild animals and the resulting 200 acres for flower gardens, the lake and parking surrounding the buildings. The interlaying lawns throughout the grounds were sown in beautiful bluegrass, making it what many people described as the most alluring spot in the entire South. Thousands of visitors from the surrounding area flocked to this dazzling

A professional baseball team was once an integral part of Soldiers' Home sporting activities. *Courtesy of the Archives of Appalachia, East Tennessee State University, Burr Harrison Collection.*

place throughout the week for amusement, recreation and excursion parties. One popular attraction was a professional baseball team that played there during the season. The massive grounds became both popular and functional, offering something to both servicemen and local citizens. It was a fun place to be and a definite asset to the city.

A magnificent brass band furnished daily and nightly concerts in the open air during the summer and in the impressive-looking Memorial Hall during the winter. The hall maintained a schedule of high-quality talent as entertainment for the veterans and visitors. Lying in front and immediately south was the magnificent Buffalo Mountain, lending additional attraction to scenery that was already entrancing. A first-class hotel was built on the premises and opened to the public, making it convenient for visitors to stay there for extended periods. Streetcars made scheduled stops there every fifteen minutes, going and coming between the military facility and the downtown. This permitted veterans to leave the grounds and come into the inner city for the day. By 1915, over $300,000 annually was expended in the maintenance of the home, and more than $250,000 was paid out each year in pensions.

Today, the Mountain Home Veterans Administration is a large medical operation serving numbers of service personnel, making a major impact on Johnson City's economy. Soldiers' Home truly became "A City Within a City."

THE PRODIGAL
"LADY OF THE FOUNTAIN"
COMES HOME

Residents in Johnson City prior to about 1937 may recall a picturesque bronze statue on Fountain Square, standing above a water fountain between Main and Market Streets, that became known as the "Lady of the Fountain." It faced southeast into the very heart of the city. This location was east of the railroad tracks and within a stone's throw of the property that once contained Henry Johnson's home, store, hotel and depot.

The statue was composed of two parts. A concrete base, fabricated in Lenoir City, was mounted to the ground, and the bronze statue portion was attached to the middle of the fountain. The statue, known as a "Greek Water Carrier" and sculpted by Alan George Newman, was ordered from New York City's J.L. Mott Works, which, in turn, subcontracted it to M.J. Seeling and Company of Williamsburg, New York, for fabrication. The fountain portion was circular and consisted of eight water spigots, with corresponding removable drain pans along the bottom of each that overflowed onto the ground. The pans were used to hold water for horses and small animals that frequented the downtown area. The fountain was a boon to fatigued and thirsty travelers for it allowed them to stop in the heart of Johnson City and obtain a refreshing drink from its waters.

While no official records of the statue's origin are known to exist, the general consensus is that it became a fixture in the city about 1905, soon after the Mountain Home Branch of the National Home for Disabled Volunteer Soldiers became operational. One speculation is that Johnson City Mayor James Summers and other city officials sought a means to honor Congressman Walter Preston Brownlow of Tennessee's First District, the man responsible for getting the military facility assigned to Johnson City. City officials conceived the idea of placing the decorative fountain in the busy downtown district to honor the elected official. Brownlow had compassion

The "Lady of the Fountain" statue on Fountain Square in downtown Johnson City provided a refreshing water break for pedestrians and animals. *Courtesy of the Archives of Appalachia.*

for the thousands of Union Civil War, and later Spanish-American War, veterans who, because of war injuries, had been reduced to homeless beggars. The home gave them a place to live until their unfortunate situations could be resolved. "Soldiers' Home," as it was also called, became "A City Within A City."

In the thirty-two years that the lady stood guard over the inner city, she saw a transformation of transportation—horses, horse-driven wagons, horse-drawn carriages, automobiles, trolleys, buses, cabs, trains and airplanes. When traffic flow around Fountain Square became a problem, city officials decided to take away the statue and make road alterations at the site. The "Lady of the Fountain" was abruptly removed from the square and taken less than a mile to Roosevelt Stadium on East Main Street. Although her tenure at the new location was about six years, she was hardly noticed at the new site. One reason was that the fountain was no longer functional. Unlike during her downtown reign, few people passed her each day, except those attending an occasional nearby sporting event at Roosevelt Stadium. At best, she received passing glances from attendees.

The Prodigal "Lady of the Fountain" Comes Home

Having served her purpose as a water fountain, she was dismantled in 1945, and the decorative concrete fountain portion was sent to the city dump, where it would vanish forever. Hearing the disturbing news, Alice Mountcastle Summers, widow of James Alexander Summers, the man who was instrumental in buying the statue, became aware that the impressive statue was heading for the scrap metal pile. She expeditiously approached city officials and procured the lady at a modest cost. This occurred just as workers were proceeding to cut the statue into pieces, having already damaged her foot. The lady was stored in a barn along East Watauga Avenue until 1950. Mrs. Summers's motives for wanting the beautiful lady were likely twofold: to preserve her husband's historic pride and joy and to bring life and respect back to the priceless relic.

After residing in Johnson City for thirty-six years, the statue was taken by Alice's daughter, Helen Summers Zollicoffer, three hundred miles to her new abode in Henderson, North Carolina. Here "Madam," as she became known, remained for the next twenty-two years in the family flower garden, with a small fountain added especially for their newly welcomed guest. Strangely enough, she was shipped there in an actual wooden coffin. The first order of business was to repair her badly damaged foot. A facsimile of it was made of concrete and painted bronze to match her overall color. The Zollicoffers recall the statue being treated like a member of the family. In a sense, Madam became a fountain again, with water being pumped into the vase and overflowing onto her shoulders and back into the containment basin.

Sadly, Johnson City's former center-of-attraction statue was hardly missed by local residents, partly because a new generation had emerged with little or no knowledge of her once-proud existence. Helen's son, John, had glowing memories of his mother thanking his grandmother for rescuing the noble statue from its near demise. Alice often remarked that the majestic sculpture almost became part of the city's World War II recycling efforts.

The year 1973 brought a ray of hope for the statue's return to Johnson City when her whereabouts in North Carolina became known. The local chamber of commerce attempted to negotiate with the Zollicoffer family to return her to Johnson City, but Helen's love for her Madam caused her to refuse their offer. Madam Zollicoffer was not about to leave her North Carolina home and the people who cared so much for her. A change in ownership of the lady was the catalyst that ultimately broke the ice. After Helen Zollicoffer passed away in 1979, the house was sold to Charles P. Rose. One condition of the sale of the property was that the "Lady of the Fountain" be donated without charge to Johnson City because of her historical significance. The new owner agreed to this stipulation.

A close-up of the "Lady of the Fountain" statue in 2006 after it was moved to the downtown municipal building. *Courtesy of the Bob Cox Collection.*

September 20, 1973, was a monumental day for Johnson City when its "prodigal lady" came home after an absence of twenty-two years. The lady's age was beginning to show in the form of cracks that ran down her legs. However, fortune smiled on the "Greek Water Carrier" when a Carter County high school teacher and sculptor, along with her students, restored the statue to a nearly new appearance that included a new bronze leg. After residing at the Mayne Williams Public Library for a period of years, the statue has been on loan or in temporary storage until a permanent and safe location can be determined.

The final chapter for the "Lady of the Fountain" has yet to be written. Hopefully, she will be restored to a place of prominence, where, once again, Johnson Citians can see her and be reminded of her storied past.

CLARENCE GREENE'S 1928

"JOHNSON CITY BLUES"

On Saturday, October 13, 1928, Frank Buckley Walker, a Columbia Records executive, came to Johnson City to record area talent for the purpose of producing old-time music on then-trendy, highly breakable, ten-inch, 78 rpm, non-stereo records. The executive soon became pleasantly surprised at the results of his Southern United States hunt.

The company announced a visit to the city with an advertisement in the October 9, 1928 edition of the *Johnson City Staff-News* that read, "Can You Sing or Play Old-Time Music?" The ad further challenged nearby aspiring recording stars to participate in an audition being held at an itinerant recording studio in the Brading-Marshall Lumber Company at 334 East Main Street on Saturday, between the hours of 9:00 a.m. and 5:00 p.m. Columbia was not the only record company making these transitory profit-seeking visits throughout the Southern states. Okeh, Victor, jointly owned Brunswick/Vocalion and Gennett labels made similar trips between 1925 and 1932. The competition was piggybacking off Ralph Peer's successful ventures in Bristol, Atlanta, Chicago and St. Louis, where he discovered the likes of Fiddlin' John Carson and Ernest V. "Pop" Stoneman.

Those fortunate individuals who passed Walker's talent standards were scheduled for a recording session between Monday and Thursday of the following week. Compensation was a one-time cash payment that authorized the company to release the songs to a hungry, record-buying public. Payouts were initially about twenty-five dollars per cut—a good deal of money in those days. The offer would soon be embellished to include royalties of two and a half cents per song.

One name that stands out prominently in the first Johnson City sessions is Clarence Greene, who lived just over the hills in Western North Carolina. He soloed and played guitar on two recordings that day: "Johnson City Blues"

The famous Columbia Records ad that appeared in the October 12, 1928 edition of the *Johnson City Staff-News. Courtesy of the Microfilm Library, East Tennessee State University.*

and "Ninety-Nine Years In Jail." The blues song became an instant hit in East Tennessee because of its references to Johnson Citians, whom the vocalist says are "the finest bunch of people in the State of Tennessee." At the conclusion of the five-stanza song, the singer laments that he is tired of roaming around and vows to return some day to the city that he loves so much.

Facts concerning the career of Clarence Horton Greene come from his son, Clarence Howard Greene, a prolific old-time and bluegrass musician and songwriter in his own right who also teaches guitar, mandolin, fiddle (longbow) and banjo (three-finger style). The younger Clarence once played music with his father and accompanied him to festivals all across the area.

The "Johnson City Blues" artist was born on June 26, 1894, in the small town of Cranberry Gap in Mitchell County, North Carolina (renamed Avery County in 1911 from parts of Caldwell, Mitchell and Watauga Counties). He resided in Johnson City during his early days, before he was married, but he was in and out of the city a good bit while on the road touring. Music came to Clarence naturally. Elbert Pritchard, on his mother's side of the family, was a blind fiddle player, and Baxter Greene, Clarence's brother, played the fiddle. Another brother was a guitarist.

Clarence Greene's 1928 "Johnson City Blues"

Greene Brothers String Band, Cranberry, North Carolina, circa 1915. *From left to right*: Baxter Greene (Clarence's brother, fiddle), Grover and Virge Greene (not related to Clarence, fiddle and banjo) and Clarence Greene (guitar). *Courtesy of Clarence Howard Greene.*

Since Johnson City is just a short distance over the mountains from Cranberry Gap, a possible route that Clarence might have traveled en route to Johnson City was the Tweetsie (East Tennessee and Western North Carolina) Railroad from Cranberry, North Carolina. He even wrote a song, "The Train That Never Returned," about the narrow-gauge railway system. Walter Davis, who later played with Clarence and a man named Jay McCool in nearby Black Mountain, were members of a band called the Mount Mitchell Ramblers. Walter was a good guitar player who, in later years, played the five-string banjo.

Clarence cited a tale that his father once beat Jimmie Rodgers, the "Father of Country Music," in a guitar-picking contest. He believes the rumor has some validity since the famous "Blue Yodel" entertainer once lived in Asheville, not far from where the Greene family lived. Clarence frequently performed at the Apple Festival in Hendersonville, his band having won that contest several times.

Greene tells a humorous story about his famous father that was oft told by family members over the years. Shortly after he recorded the two songs for Columbia Records, he left the city for several weeks on a musical tour. During his absence, a rumor began circulating around town that the thirty-four-year-old musician had passed away. When the unsuspecting Clarence returned home, he strolled into an East Main Street record shop that is believed to have been J.G. Sterchi Furniture Company at 222–26 East Main. In addition to furniture, they sold regular and player pianos; Victrola, Brunswick and Edison phonographs; and records. The music attendant, surprised to see the musician walk through the door, told him that the buzz around the city was that he was deceased. Amused, he informed Clarence that his records began selling better when people thought he was dead.

Clarence participated in another recording session during the 1928 Columbia visit. This time he teamed up with the Wise Brothers for two instrumental songs: "Pride of the Ball" and "Kitty Waltz." The trio consisted of Clarence (fiddle), Bee Wise (banjo) and Omer Wise Sr. (guitar). Almost exactly one year later, Frank Walker returned a second time to Johnson City for another talent audition. Many of the people who had performed for the first session showed up for the second one. By this time, Clarence was playing music with an assemblage known as Byrd (William B.) Moore and His Hot Shots.

The first record contained two songs, "Careless Love" and "Three Men Went A Hunting." The second one included "Frankie Silvers" and "The Hills of Tennessee." Performers were Clarence Greene (fiddle, tenor vocal), Tom Ashley (guitar, lead vocal) and Byrd Moore (guitar, baritone vocal). Moore sang lead on "The Hills of Tennessee." According to Clarence:

> Byrd Moore was from Norton, Virginia. He and my dad knew each other and played music together from years back. Although he was a barber by trade, whenever he got ready to play music, he closed the barbershop and left. He spent a lot of his money on new clothes, always wearing a new suit and hat. He went by the unusual nickname of "hog." "Johnson City Blues" is very similar to another song, "Chattanooga Blues." Dad had heard that song from the Allen Brothers after they recorded it in Atlanta in 1927. Dad was present when they recorded it and probably picked up the tune and a few words for "Johnson City Blues."

The senior Clarence received a letter from Jim Walsh, former record collector and editor of *Hobbies Magazine*, about 1951. Walsh requested a copy of the tragedy song, "Frankie Silvers." Frankie "Frances" Silvers was an eighteen-year-old mountain girl who lived on the Toe River in North Carolina and notoriously became the first white woman in the state to be hanged. She was convicted of killing her husband on December 22, 1831. Many stories have circulated over the ages as to the proof of her guilt or innocence, but time has blurred the account to the extent that the truth will likely never be

Clarence Greene's 1928 "Johnson City Blues"

Byrd Moore's Hot Shots, Johnson City, Tennessee. *From left to right*: Byrd Moore, Clarence Greene and Tom Ashley. *Courtesy of Clarence Howard Greene.*

known. Like many tragedies of that era, such as Floyd Collins's mine accident, the event made its way onto a record that helped secure its place in history.

Johnson City was not the only city where the senior Greene made records; he had the distinction of having recorded twenty-eight songs during six sessions for eleven record labels. A couple of the ARC (American Record Company) sides were never released. His first session occurred on November 5, 1927, in Atlanta, Georgia, where he recorded two songs: "On the Banks of the Ohio" and "Fond Affection." Clarence (vocal, guitar) teamed up with Will Abernathy (autoharp, harmonica) for the recordings. The pair then joined an unknown assemblage, the Blue Ridge Singers, for two additional selections: "I Want to Go There Don't You?" and "Glory Is Now Rising In My Soul." On both songs, Clarence played guitar but did not vocalize.

Clarence also participated in the Victor Sessions organized by Ralph Peer in Bristol, Tennessee, on October 30, 1928, just two weeks after the first Johnson City Sessions, putting on disc two additional numbers: "Good-Night Darling" and "Little Bunch of Roses." This time, he soloed on vocal and guitar. The record producer insisted on original songs for this gathering.

A fourth opportunity arose for Clarence. This time he traveled to Richmond, Indiana, and cut two discs, "Cincinnati Rag" and "Pig Angle,"

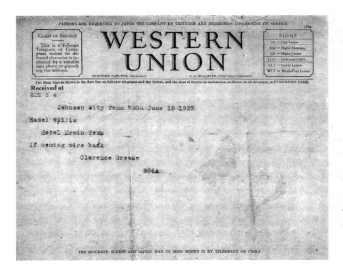

A Western Union Telegram addressed to the Hotel Erwin, dated June 15, 1929, from Clarence Greene to Hazel Willis, his second wife. *Courtesy of Clarence Howard Greene.*

on February 13, 1930, for the Champion and Superior labels, jointly owned by the Starr Piano Company. On the former selection, the duo was known as Moore and Greene, but on the latter one, they were listed as Moss and Long. Other songs recorded at the Richmond session were never issued.

The last session that the entertainer attended was in New York City between November 30 and December 2, 1931, for Art Satherly of the American Record Company. By this time, Clarence was playing music with the Blue Ridge Mountain Entertainers consisting of Clarence (fiddle, vocals), Tom Ashley (guitar, vocals), Gwin Foster (guitar, harmonica), Walter Davis (guitar) and Will Abernathy (autoharp, harmonica). Songs included "Penitentiary Bound," "Drunk Man Blues," "Crooked Creek Blues," "Short Life of Trouble," "Baby All Night Long," "Cincinnati Breakdown," "Honeysuckle Rag," "Over at Tom's House," "The Fiddler's Contest," "Washington and Lee Swing," "Goodnight Waltz," "I have No Loving Mother Now," "Corrine, Corrina" and "Bring me a Leaf From the Sea." The company issued the songs using other names, such as Tom Ashley, Ashley and Greene, Walter Davis and Ashley and Foster. They were also pressed on seven additional record labels: Conqueror, Romeo, Oriole, Banner, Vocalion, Perfect and Melotone.

The younger Clarence remembers when country music historians Archie Green and Ed Kahn came to Penland, North Carolina, in 1960 and again in 1961 to interview his father. This was just prior to a visit Archie made with Fiddlin' Charlie Bowman, another participant on the two Johnson City Sessions, in Union City, Georgia. Clarence asked Archie, "What did Charlie

Clarence Greene's 1928 "Johnson City Blues"

Bowman do for you? He's a monkey," referring to the fiddler's comedic personality. He could not recall Archie's response. Clarence went on to say:

> *I cannot remember ever visiting Johnson City with my Dad. We didn't have a car then so we didn't travel too much outside the local area. I was about fourteen years old before I was able to play music with him. He wanted to go to Johnson City but did not go there much in later years. I can recall that he once stayed in and around Elizabethton a good bit back in the old days. There was a place there called Cat Island and is referred to on one of Tom Ashley's records made as a skit in 1931 supposedly recorded at Tom's house, but in actuality it was made in New York. The flip side is "Fiddler's Convention."*

The senior Clarence singled out Dedrick Harris as an inspiration and as the best fiddle player around. The fiddler was a participant in the now-famous 1925 Mountain City Fiddler's Convention. He had a twin brother, Demp, who accompanied him to the contest. Clarence was of the opinion that Fiddlin' John Carson was more skilled as an entertainer than as a fiddler, believing his group recordings had more overall listening appeal than his solo fiddling and vocal arrangements.

Over his lifetime, Greene worked in local mica plants, did spar mining and was a construction worker at one time. He never had one job for any length of time; instead, he worked several jobs over the years. Regardless of his vocation, he always found time to play the music that he loved. Clarence recalled one incident with Frank Walker:

> *On the Byrd Moore recording session, Columbia paid the performer a flat rate for a side but did not pay royalties. Dad told a tale to Ed Kahn and Archie Green during his interview with them. When they did that session with Byrd Moore and the Hot Shots, Frank was there and had them do a test record. Frank commented that they sounded great and wanted them to proceed to do a master record of the song. Back then records were cut in wax. Dad was the group's finance person so he told Frank that before they cut the master, they needed to talk about finances. Frank said they were familiar how his company operated. Dad told them they were not going to record the song for the price being offered and asked for more money from the record company. Frank said that there was no way they could pay them more. Clarence turned to the band and told them to start casing their instruments because they were wasting time and could be playing music somewhere and making money. The musicians proceeded to leave the building and then*

Clarence Greene playing for a square dance at Penland School of Crafts about 1940. *Courtesy of Clarence Howard Greene.*

were called back in by Walker. The producer had had a change of heart. Surprisingly, for cutting four sides, the group was paid about $900, which was good money in 1929. Dad said the money was put in a satchel and that it was "plum full of money." Dad repeated that story several times over the years.

Clarence played music right to the end of his life, routinely playing for square dances, including Geneva Hall in Little Switzerland on Saturday nights. His son used to go with him in the days when his band was called the Toe River Valley Boys. He began playing with the group after his father died. They performed two different festivals at East Tennessee State University in 1966–67, and the younger Clarence recalled that Flatt and Scruggs were at one and Doc Watson was at the other. Janette Carter Jett also played there.

The "Johnson City Blues" singer passed away on October 22, 1961, at the age of sixty-seven and was buried in Bear Creek Cemetery near Ledger, North Carolina, not far from Bakersville. Although death silenced Clarence Horton Greene, this legendary musician lives on through his songs to entertain new generations of old-time music lovers and to proclaim to the world his love for Johnson City and "the finest bunch of people in the State of Tennessee."

THE BIZARRE ACCOUNT OF AN
ELEPHANT HANGING

A traveling circus always spelled excitement for young and old during the golden days of yesteryear. On September 12, 1916, the Sparks Brothers Circus rolled into Kingsport, Tennessee, on ten railcars with advertised upcoming appearances in the Model City, Johnson City and Erwin. It had previously played in St. Paul, Virginia, in the Clinch River Valley. A poster from that distant era described its entertainment value:

> *A Tremendous Exhibition of Wealth and Splendor—Perfect Specimens of The Earth's Most Curious Creatures Gathered Together into One Immense Menagerie—The Champions of All Countries Compete in Feats of Daring and Grace—The Princely Salaries Paid by This Mammoth Enterprise Have Robbed All Europe of Their Most Valuable Artists— Male and Female Riders, Aerial Artists, Leapers, Tumblers, Gymnasts and Sensational Death Defying Feats of Skill and Daring by Both Male and Female Performers—A Big Troupe Of High School Horses and Immense Herd of Wonderfully Trained Elephants, Two Groups of Forest-Bred, Man-Killing Lions Performing in Great Steel Enclosures.*

The colorful circus poster also contained an eye-grabbing entry: "Mary —The Largest Living Land Animal on Earth." She was said to be three inches taller than Jumbo and weighed over five tons. The magnificent pachyderm was the pride and joy of owner Charlie Sparks. Being a relatively small traveling show, unlike the much larger John Robinson Circus, Sparks needed a cash cow as a drawing card to bring in customers and revenue to fill all five thousand seats in his massive tent. The thirty-year-old Mary filled that bill, at least until mid-September 1916. An event would happen during those three unforgettable city meetings that would continue to be talked about to this day. Johnson City found itself in the crossfire between the initial problem and the final solution.

Although few, if any, people alive today will remember the well-publicized incident, media coverage would not let the story die in the almost one hundred years since it happened. The principle character was Mary, a large, well-trained elephant valued at $425,000 that astonished the masses during the tours, playing baseball with a .400 batting average and producing twenty-five tunes on musical horns without striking a single sour note. With all her impressive credentials, nevertheless, Mary's record was blemished in that she had previously caused the death of two people. The elephant's trainer was twenty-three-year-old Red Eldridge, a slight-of-build railroad drifter with flaming red hair who had been employed on the job just two days. Although he was inexperienced in managing such a hefty animal, he was assigned the important role of being Mary's animal handler while she marched in the noon parade in Kingsport.

What happened on that momentous day to turn Mary from a submissive, peaceful animal into a murderous, angry beast? Several theories abound, but the primary one was that, while Red was riding in the parade atop the massive pachyderm, Mary spotted a partially eaten, discarded watermelon rind lying on the road. Eager to consume it, she abruptly stopped and halted the parade. In an effort to get Mary and the procession moving again, Red hooked her ear with a sharp metal hook that was attached to his trainer's stick. This would prove to be a grave mistake. Apparently, Mary did not take too kindly to Red's admonition and began resisting him. Suddenly, and without warning, the big animal wrapped her trunk firmly around her trainer's body and tossed him ten feet in the air, causing him to come crashing to the ground. As if that were not enough, she gored her poor keeper with her sharp tusks, crushed his head with her heavy foot, picked up his now lifeless body and hurled him against the side of a concession stand, knocking the side out of it.

The horrified crowd became enraged by the elephant's sudden actions. Allegedly, several men in the crowd whipped out their revolvers and fired at the elephant, including a nearby blacksmith, Hench Cox, who shot Mary five times with his .32–20 pistol. Unlike today, the carrying of firearms by individuals in 1916 was acceptable and widely practiced. Their actions did little more than annoy the big beast. Charlie Sparks was faced with a momentous dilemma. He could spare Mary's life and risk the possibility of other cities banning the elephant from entering their premises, fearing a similar incident in their towns, or he could put the critter to death and search for another cash cow attraction. Although the decision was not an easy one,

The Bizarre Account of an Elephant Hanging

Charlie felt that he was left with but one option: Mary had to be destroyed and it had to be done soon. Without the benefit of a trial by an impartial jury, Mary was summarily sentenced to death. What remained to be determined was the method to be deployed in carrying out her execution.

Sparks also had knowledge that Johnson City, where his show was scheduled to appear next, had passed a privilege-tax ordinance restricting a carnival's operations within city limits. This move was designed to protect area citizens from being swindled by unscrupulous sideshow operators. As valuable as Mary had been to the circus, it was time for her to make her final bow if the diminutive Sparks Brothers Circus was to remain in business. Being a circus man, Sparks decided to profit from the tragic situation and make the hanging a public display. "Why not," he reasoned, "take advantage of an unfortunate event?"

The circus concluded its performances in Kingsport and moved to Erwin, Tennessee, for the second leg of its three-city tour. Several ideas immediately surfaced as to how to destroy Mary. Reportedly, an attempt to electrocute her using forty-four thousand volts of electricity brought a slight reaction from her, but failed to accomplish its ultimate goal. Some individuals challenged that statement because they said there were no cables in the railroad yards with that much current. Another consideration was the use of two trains going in opposite directions to literally rip her apart or, conversely, have two trains plow into her and crush her. Neither selection appeared feasible and both were, at best, risky. Charlie Davis, superintendent of the Clinchfield yards, was given the daunting task of making preparations for Mary's demise. He conceived the novel idea of using a railway derrick to hang Mary, an idea that he reasoned would draw a sizable crowd. After consulting Sam Bondurant, derrick foreman, about the idea, the two of them agreed that this was the most logical way to proceed.

At the next day's matinee, Mary was conspicuously absent from the show; instead, she was securely chained outside the circus tent. Witnesses remembered that she swayed nervously while the show was going on inside, as if aware of her upcoming fate. During the acts, the ringmaster announced that Mary would be hanged in the Clinchfield railroad yard that afternoon. Everyone was invited to witness the event at no additional charge. The hanging of Murderous Mary was to become an event that rivaled anything that could be conjured up under the big circus tent. An estimated twenty-five hundred spectators arrived at six o'clock on a drizzly evening in the Erwin rail yards near the powerhouse for the hanging, which fittingly turned into a circus-like atmosphere. Reportedly, Sparks brought in his other elephants as an added attraction and lined them, trunk to tail, to witness the hanging,

The only known photo of the infamous elephant hanging in Erwin, Tennessee. *Courtesy of the Archives of Appalachia, East Tennessee State University, Unicoi County Collection.*

The Bizarre Account of an Elephant Hanging

as if to warn them of the potential consequences of any improper behavior from them.

At the appointed time, Mary was escorted into the Clinchfield railroad yards, where a wrecking derrick was waiting. The time had come for her execution. Prior to the hanging, circus officials removed her massive tusks, as evidenced by them being missing in the only known picture of the elephant hanging. A seven-eighths-inch chain was placed firmly around her neck. As the derrick began to slowly raise the elephant off the ground, initially nothing happened. But when the noose began to tighten, Mary struggled from her precarious circumstances, jerking sharply and causing the chain to break, proving that an undersized chain is no match for a ten-thousand-pound elephant. She fell helplessly to the ground, breaking a hip, but still managing to sit up. A frightened crowd momentarily scattered for cover, afraid of the now powerless and pitiful creature. One witness remembered that the ground shook when Mary fell.

A speedy decision was made to repeat the process after replacing the broken chain with a larger one. The execution was delayed while a crew was hurriedly sent out to locate one. Upon their return, the operation was repeated, and this time the execution went off without a hitch. One witness revealed that the ill-fated Mary kicked momentarily and then became motionless, indicating that the end was quick and merciful. Her body remained aloft on the derrick for thirty minutes, perhaps to ensure that she was dead and possibly to allow time for people to get a close view of her. The now lifeless elephant was lowered to the ground, where a steam shovel picked up the remains and took them to a nearby gravesite. Circus workers had dug an enormous grave for their once-prized circus star along the railroad tracks, not far from the derrick. No marker was ever placed at the makeshift grave, nor were any flowers laid there. Since the exact location of her final resting place was never recorded, the whereabouts of Mary's remains can only be speculated. A few old-timers from the area, who either witnessed the event or were told of her gravesite, still point to a particular spot in the train yard to indicate where Mary's remains lie.

Today, newcomers to the area have trouble believing the story of the hanging, but the account has received much local and national publicity over the years, including a story in a Chicago daily newspaper. Another mention of it was in 1938, in the popular Robert Ripley's "Believe It Or Not" column (King Features Syndicate, Inc.). The astonishing story, while the specifics may have blurred, enhanced or even misrepresented over time, is an undisputed fact. An elephant was hanged in Erwin, Tennessee, on September 13, 1916.

THE DREADFUL NEWSPAPER HEADLINE: "OUR BOB IS DEAD"

An old, undated copy of Johnson City's local, weekly, turn-of-the-century newspaper, the *Comet*—the very publication that Bob Taylor founded and edited—once recalled when the beloved Johnson City native and former governor resigned from politics after a stellar political career. The popular elected official quit the field of public service on his retirement from the gubernatorial chair in 1899, only to be given a new lease by the people the next year. In "quitting" the world of politics, the always-witty Taylor expressed his feelings about his long and illustrious career in characteristic style:

> *I am about to shuffle off this mortal coil of politics and fly away to the haven of my native mountains, where I may think and dream in peace, safe from the sickening sting of unjust criticism; safe from the talons of some old political vulture; safe from the slimy kiss and keen dagger of ingratitude. I do not mean to say that all politicians are vultures or that they are all hypocrites or assassins; for the great majority of our public men are upright and honest, and worthy of the confidence reposed in them by the people; yet there are black wings in the political firmament and reptiles crawl and hiss in every capitol.*
>
> *But, thank God, the live thunders of eternal truth always clear the atmosphere and the heel of justice will surely bruise the serpent's head. I do not retire from this office with the ranking of disappointment and chagrin in my bosom, but rather as one who retires from labor to rest, from war to peace, from trouble to happiness. I do not retire, the somnambulist of a shattered dream, but with all the buds of hope bursting into bloom, and all the bowers of the future ringing with melody. I am contented with my lot in life. Three times I have worn the laurel wreath of honor, twined by the people of my native state, and that is glory enough for me.*

The *Comet* newspaper, initially a weekly publication, later became a daily one and operated from early 1884 to about 1919. *Courtesy of the Microfilm Library, East Tennessee State University.*

While I believe that the good in politics outweighs the bad, yet how thorny is the path and how unhappy the pilgrimage to him who dares to do his duty. There are no flowers, except a few bouquets snatched from the graves of fallen foes; there is no happiness except the transient thrill of cruel triumph, which passes like a shadow across the heart. Every honest man who runs for office is a candidate for trouble, for the fruits of political victory turn to ashes on the lips. To me, there is nothing in this world so pathetic as a candidate.

He is like a mariner without a compass, drifting on the tempest-tossed waves of uncertainty between the smiling cliffs of hope and the frowning crags of fear. He is a walking petition and a living prayer; he is the packhorse of public sentiment; he is the dromedary of politics. And even if he reaches the goal of his ambition, he will soon feel the beak of the vulture in his heart and the fang of the serpent in his soul.

Governor Taylor made reference to the great flood and Mount Ararat from Genesis 8 in the Bible when he stated:

I am no longer a candidate. Never again will I be inaugurated into public office. The ark of my humble public career now rests on the Ararat of public life, and I stand on its peaceful summit and look down on the receding floor of politics. The dove of my destiny has brought me an olive branch from happier fields and I go hence to labor and to love. I take with me a heart full of gratitude and a soul full of precious memories—gratitude to the people for their unwavering confidence in me—precious memories of my friends, who have been kind and true.

The record I have made is an open book to all. I am willing to live by that record. I am willing to die by it. For whatever mistakes I may have committed, I have kept steadily in view the honor of the State and the happiness of the people.

The Dreadful Newspaper Headline: "Our Bob Is Dead"

A sketch of Governor Bob Taylor as drawn by Junior High School student Earl Hunt, from a May 29, 1934 graduating class student project publication. *Courtesy of the Archives of Appalachia, East Tennessee State University, Pat Watson Collection.*

The same newspaper that announced his retirement from politics a few years earlier shocked the state and nation on March 31, 1912, by publicly announcing, "Our Bob is Dead." There was absolutely no question to whom the article was referring; there was only one "Our Bob." Upon every hearthstone in Tennessee, this weighty announcement fell with the heaviness of personal mourning. Tears flowed like rivers from the eyes of those whose hearts were pierced by the awful news. This elected official was truly loved and appreciated by thousands. The publication went on to summarize the career of a man whose standing was on the same respected footing as the founder of Johnson City, Henry Johnson. In 1884, Mr. Taylor was selected as presidential elector of the Democratic National Convention, which nominated Grover Cleveland for the presidency of the United States. The paper further stated the details of the governor and senator's passing:

Born July 31, 1850, Robert Love Taylor, senior United States Senator from Tennessee, has passed from among men. His soul took its flight at 9:40 this morning at Providence Hospital in Washington, DC, to which institution Senator Taylor was carried Wednesday night and where an operation for gallstones was performed Thursday morning.

Death stilled his good and noble heart in a room that overlooked a little park whose reviving symbols of life and resurrection and message of gladness to mankind he was wont to interpret in eloquent tongue.

For three days he has looked with dimming eyes upon that little square whose budding grass, swelling boughs and bursting buds are in joyous response to the warmth of spring's sunshine. It was an ideal day—just such a day that the lips now forever dumb have so many times described in words of matchless eloquence and beautiful meaning.

It was a glorious day for "Our Bob" to take final leave of a world into which he poured a wealth of cheer and happiness and sunshine. It was as if God had mercifully given his genial soul as an escort the tender beauties of an ideal spring day.

There is a reverent suggestion of the eternal fitness of things for Bob Taylor to pass from earth amid the splendors of a perfect day for his buoyant and happy spirit to return to its Maker on the breath of a glorious morning.

Senator Taylor began to sink following the operation Thursday morning, lapsing into unconsciousness at three o'clock in the morning and he passed away without having regained consciousness even for a minute.

There were present at the bedside when the final summons came Mrs. Taylor, worn and wan, from a racking vigil of three days and nights; her brother, Charles St. John of Virginia; Mrs. Sam Williamson, a lifelong friend; and Dr. Harrison Cook. Mrs. Taylor is so unnerved from the shock of the overwhelming grief that she is under medical care at the hospital.

Bob had to weight the risk associated with an operation. He was not in favor of it but relented after his physicians offered positive yet frank statements that such an operation was absolutely imperative. But he had waited too long. The terrific suffering accompanying the passage of the gallstones had reduced his vitality and so affected his digestive organs as to preclude the chances of favorable reaction from the operation. Then too, at sixty-one, his age militated against his recovery. Senator Taylor was subject to these attacks, each recurring one leaving him weaker for another. Shortly before his departure for Nashville about six weeks ago, whither he went to discuss his impending campaign with friends.

The Dreadful Newspaper Headline: "Our Bob Is Dead"

Senator Taylor was stricken with a comparably mild attack of his old trouble. He responded to treatment in a week or ten days, but he never regained his wonted health. To friends who talked to him about his malady, Senator Taylor would impress his own disturbing realization of his condition. He seemed to have premonitions of the possibility of its fatal termination. The vague and dark foreboding naturally found expression in ways that attracted attention and some of his more intimate friends were pained to remark that his conversation and manner had lost something of their old-time flavor and piquancy.

Bob Taylor was of the stock that made Tennessee great. His father, Nathaniel G. Taylor, was of pioneer descent and the laws of heredity cut no inconsiderable figure in the making of men. He represented the First Tennessee district in Congress. Bob's mother, Emily Taylor, was a daughter of Landon C. Haynes, a Confederate senator from Tennessee who was said to be one of the most eloquent men the nation has produced. Bob entered this life in 1850, in Happy Valley, appropriately named, in Carter County near Johnson City. The Taylor home was a modest frame structure with a chimney at each end and an attic.

One publication summarized Bob's career succinctly by noting that, as a public speaker, he had few equals and far fewer superiors. As a candidate,

An old postcard depicting Governor Bob Taylor's birthplace near Milligan College, just outside of Johnson City. *Courtesy of the Bob Cox Collection.*

he won the hearts of his people by his convincing and humorous arguments, never failing to make friends for him and his cause. As a lecturer, he was always one of the most successful in the country, both financially and in winning popular favor.

DeLong Rice, friend and companion of Senator Taylor, offered a tribute to the memory of his departed buddy in words that appear to be coming from the former "War of the Roses" governor:

> *O, unique character among men. We salute thee ere we say farewell. No mind could soar in beauty's skies with freer flight. Who but thee could drop with grace from flying planets to grimacing monkeys? Who but thee could hold us spellbound with discourse on such little things as beetles and frogs and butterflies?...Would that we could hold and fix thee here in the fullness of thy wonted power, as a lasting legacy to millions yet to be; but barren is our wish, for while broken-hearted music sobbed in sacred song above they open grave, we saw all that earth can claim of thee sink to everlasting rest beneath sheaves and shocks of roses.*

Perhaps the greatest honor bestowed upon the former congressional senator was the adoption of four Senate resolutions:

> *1. That the Senate has heard with profound sorrow of the death of the Honorable Robert Love Taylor, senator from the State of Tennessee.*
> *2. That a committee of twelve senators be appointed by the Vice President to handle the funeral arrangements of the senator.*
> *3. That, as a further mark of respect, his remains be removed from Washington to Nashville, Tennessee for burial.*
> *4. That the Secretary communicate these resolutions to the House of Representatives and transmit a copy to the family of the deceased senator.*

The Senate offered one additional mark of respect when it voted to adjourn until the next day. The death of Bob Taylor was the end of a colorful era that was greatly influenced by "Our Bob."

JULY FOURTH

CELEBRATIONS WERE ONCE

BIG HAPPENINGS

The late S.R. Jennings once lived in beautiful Robins' Roost on South Roan Street in Johnson City. The stately dwelling was built by William Graham in 1890 and became the home of Governor Robert Love Taylor from 1892 to 1897. His younger brother, Al, also a governor of the state, occupied it between 1900 and 1903. Mr. Jennings made a significant contribution to Johnson City history by painting in words a vibrant picture from his memory of what it was like to celebrate July Fourth soon after the turn of the century in the downtown area. He witnessed the pageantry and splendor of the event firsthand as a youngster:

Everybody came to town that day because big doings were in the making. There was always a public parade with men and women dressed up for the occasion in decorated costumes and riding horses.

S.R. remembered when the Soldiers' Home (now known as the Veterans Administration) Band permeated the air with inspiring martial music. Parades consisted of an array of carriages, hacks and buggies, all drawn by horses that were colorfully adorned with red, white and blue streamers or other ornamentation. In later years, when technology was more advanced, Model-T Fords became the chief mode of transportation. The parade usually started in midmorning and lasted well past the noon hour. Afterward, political leaders gave speeches, usually at Fountain Square or other areas large enough to hold the horde of residents and visitors. According to Jennings:

These were orators in the old-time style. They were long-winded all right; spoke for two or three hours. People didn't think they were much good if they couldn't hold forth that long and felt cheated otherwise.

CELEBRATE
WEDNESDAY
JULY 4
IN
JOHNSON CITY

A 1906 July Fourth advertisement from the *Comet* announcing the upcoming citywide celebration. *Courtesy of the Microfilm Library, East Tennessee State University.*

For many, the best part of the day was enjoying a scrumptious basket lunch that had been prepared earlier at home. Normal fare included such delicacies as fried chicken, pies stacked one on top of another, cakes, homemade pickles, cold biscuits or a round of light bread, complete with a knife for slicing it. Enterprising individuals prepared lemonade and sold it to the crowd. Since keeping ice on hand in the July heat was virtually impossible, vendors had an imaginative scheme for selling their product. They obtained a three-gallon bucket, sliced and squeezed lemons in it, added an appropriate amount of sugar and then let the concoction soak until time for use. When a customer appeared desiring a cool drink, the seller simply mixed the sweet lemony concentrate with cold refreshing water that had recently been drawn from one of several downtown springs and kept in the shade. Most patrons drank the invigorating beverage at the stand from the same metal cup without any thought of ingesting germs or anyone becoming ill.

Jennings recalled that about 1909, when the Ringling Brothers Circus came to Johnson City on the Fourth, an exciting new dimension was added to the festivities. People streamed into town from all over neighboring counties. Between the First and Second World Wars, parades and fireworks were still a significant ingredient of July Fourth celebrations, but political speeches dwindled somewhat. People began lavishly decorating their homes and shooting their own fireworks. Some local churches chose this day for their annual church picnics. Many people packed food baskets and took rides on the Tweetsie Railroad to Elk Park, riding in open-air excursion cars that featured a long bench in the center with seats on both sides that offered magnificent views of the surrounding area.

A newspaper from 1926 states that the National Sanatorium had three types of races as part of its celebration—sack, lighted candle and potato. After the sun had set at the end of the long, patriotic day, a fireworks display signaled the finale of the activities. Jennings recalled being in a large field and watching rockets ascend into the sky and then explode, causing the crowd to jump at the noise and exclaim with delight over the light display.

Afterward, tired and sleepy families climbed back onto their wagons and buggies and returned home. Another successful celebration of our country's birthday had come and gone.

CONFESSIONS OF A YOUTHFUL, GRAVEL-FLIPPING SHARPSHOOTER

Young Donnie Bowman was known within miles of his family's early 1800s, two-story log house as a skilled gravel-flipping man. Born in 1916, the fourth of ten siblings, the youngster acquired a talent that would evoke the pride of family members and the envy of neighbors and friends.

While he was about fourteen years old, Donnie developed the talent of hunting with what locals around East Tennessee referred to as a gravel flipper, a device known as a slingshot in most parts of the country. His talent also included making high-quality gravel flippers. People all around the community begged him to make one for them, and he usually complied. Donnie's sharp eye and quick reflexes brought many a rabbit and squirrel to its final destiny on his family's dining room table, to the delight of his mother, Fannie. He made it a practice to never venture far from home without having a gravel flipper attached securely to his belt. The weapon was so essential to him that, when he went into the woods looking for small game, he usually carried a spare just in case one broke. Hunting was not just a recreational pastime with the youngster; it was much more than that. As a young lad growing up in the 1920s and '30s, he also brought home rabbits and squirrels to be used as barter at a nearby country store for other necessary items around the household. This was especially significant during the dark Depression years.

One of Bowman's cherished memories occurred while he was attending Gray Station School. As with most schoolhouses of that era, a potbellied stove provided heat for the classroom. One school chore was for two boys, near the end of the school day, to go outside and bring a supply of pre-cut logs back to the classroom for use the next day. As customary, Donnie had his gravel flipper with him hidden in his shirt bosom. As he and another student were making their way back to the building with some logs, they spotted a

Charlie and Fannie Bowman raised twelve children in this century-old, two-story log house in Gray's Station. Young Donnie is shown third from the right. *Courtesy of the Charlie Bowman Collection.*

covey of quail scampering nearby. Donnie's response was automatic and natural. He hurriedly fetched his trusty old flipper, grabbed some pebbles from his pocket and, within seconds, had three quail lying motionless on the ground. But this caused a slight dilemma for the youthful lad. If he left the birds outside, stray dogs might drag them off before school was dismissed. If he carried them inside, his teacher was certain to object and make him take them back outside. His solution was to carefully position each one inside his shirt and return to the classroom with the supply of firewood. He sat in his seat with his arms folded lightly over his chest, silently concealing the birds that would soon be his evening meal. When the final school bell rang, the young sharpshooter dashed out of the building and ran home with his prized catch.

Donnie had warmhearted memories of his old rabbit-hunting canine, Buster, which he described as being a mixture of bulldog and rat terrier. He would later say that this dog was faster than any in the community. It was Buster's responsibility to locate the downed animal and bring it back to its master. Buster was so dedicated to Donnie that he followed him to school most days and stayed there until it was time for him to escort him home. Unknown to his mother, Donnie had the curious habit of laying his jacket down in the field for his best friend to lie on until classes were over. He took advantage of the two-mile journey home for some hunting. It was not unusual for him to bring two or three rabbits home to a waiting, delighted mother. Sometimes Donnie would take his catch to Sid Martin Store and sell them for ten cents apiece. Over time, the commodity increased to a quarter. Rather than take cash, the lad often swapped the animals for marbles or shotgun shells. While he occasionally used his shotgun for hunting, it was his gravel flipper that gave him the greatest enjoyment and usually his most bountiful catch. His ammunition consisted of specially chosen small rocks that earned him a reputation for his skill with the gravel shooter—not just any rock would do the job.

The flippers that Bowman used were never store-bought or haphazardly fabricated. He made them by going into the woods and finding that special dogwood tree limb that offered the best natural fork for the flipper. No other tree offered a better quality of wood than that species. He knew which ones to remove and use and which ones to ignore. Donnie's next step was to obtain rubber for the sling; again, that had to be carefully selected. His supplier was the nearby Ed Adams Garage. The owner usually offered him a discarded inner tube from an automobile. As Donnie approached adulthood, he found it increasingly difficult to locate inner tubes with the proper rubber content. Newer ones consisted of synthetic rubber and did not yield proper stretch qualities needed for the sling. Although rocks were a natural choice for flippers, ball bearings from old cars made good projectiles. They shot like bullets but rarely penetrated the victim, often allowing the bearing to be located nearby and reused. This was important because of the limited supply of spent ball bearings obtainable. The final step in making a flipper was to fabricate the pad that held the pellet. This was cut from worn-out shoes that had been handed down through several children and were ready to be discarded. Donnie, being a true craftsman, stressed that the leather had to be high quality or the flipper would not be accurate.

Bowman and a small group of neighborhood boys went rabbit hunting on Saturdays and weekdays after the farm chores were finished. Each youngster brought his favorite dog, but according to Donnie, none could compare with Buster, which always outdid the others. Donnie's sister, Pauline, once told a tale on her brother. Her husband, Bill Huggans, was from New York and wanted to go hunting with Donnie because he had heard of his reputation as a skilled gravel-flipping hunter. He bought shells from Niles Gray at London Hardware Company in downtown Johnson City. Niles, a friend of the Bowman family, cautioned Bill that if he was going hunting with Donnie, all he needed was a gravel flipper. Bill had no idea what he was talking about, so the amused Niles offered further explanation to the visiting Yankee.

Bowman's recollection of the best hunt he ever experienced was on a Saturday with area residents Sherman Adams and Hobart Hale. The pair were grown men and carried twelve-gauge shotguns. Donnie, who was much younger, brought only his trusty gravel flipper along. It was a blustery cold day, with just enough snow on the ground to adequately track animals. By this time, rabbits could be sold for twenty-five cents apiece. The hunt went forward as planned and ended with a predictable outcome. Donnie and Buster snagged eleven rabbits; Adams killed three; and Hale managed but one. As the trio was leaving, a rabbit unexpectedly ran out of a bush and Donnie had him before the other two men realized it was there. That increased his take to an even dozen and further added to the chagrin of his companions. A simple, crudely built gravel flipper had won out over two high-quality shotguns, but everyone knew the reason was because of the shooters rather than their weapons.

Another amusing story involved area resident Bill Hunt, a schoolteacher who grew up working on a nearby farm. A chicken hawk kept snatching away his chickens. He was determined to bring it down, but so far had been unsuccessful. Once, while Donnie was visiting at his house, a woman began screaming that the dreaded bird had returned overhead. While several men ran to get their weapons, the hawk unobtrusively landed in a nearby tree. The men returned fully armed and began shooting randomly at the feathered animal. This caused the bird to leave the tree and fly near Bowman, which was a fatal mistake. Donnie carefully placed a piece of gravel in his flipper, took quick aim and brought the hawk to the ground to the amazement of the other men.

Bowman recalls working on a neighbor's farm for a full day just for the privilege of borrowing the owner's shotgun to go hunting the next day. The hunt ended with his shooting a rabbit and a quail, a result far short of his usual quota. He realized he needed to stay with the weapon that was responsible for his reputation as a huntsman. On the next outing, he wisely took along only his gravel flipper.

Fannie regularly cooked squirrel meat and gravy at the old log home. She prepared one average-sized squirrel for each of four people that she planned to serve. The family of twelve, which included two adults and ten hungry kids, required three full-sized squirrels. The Bowman youngsters were responsible for skinning, cleaning and removing hairs from the animals. Fannie had a firm rule: if she saw even one hair on it, she would not cook it until it was removed. Several of Donnie's siblings recall how Fannie prepared the squirrel for a meal. Initially, she cut about six or seven pieces of meat from each squirrel, placed them in a pot, covered them with water and boiled the meat until it was tender. Squirrel meat is tough and has to be tested frequently. After removing the meat from the pot of water, she saved the hot broth for making gravy. She next coated the meat with flour that had been seasoned with salt and pepper and placed it in a hot cast-iron skillet of lard, where it fried until it was golden brown on both sides. She covered the pot with a lid and cooked it at reduced heat for another twenty minutes or until it appeared done. She then removed the meat from the skillet. Next came gravy preparation. She prepared it in the same skillet as the meat. After pouring off about half of the fat, she added the broth to the skillet, along with a mixture of milk and flour, and stirred the contents until they thickened. The contents were allowed to boil. The brown bits that formed on the bottom of the pan were scraped loose into the gravy. These tasty morsels were what gave the gravy such a delightful flavor.

Fannie's final step was to serve the meat and gravy, along with some homemade biscuits, to her impatient, hungry family. If anyone had paid attention to the gravel-flipping boy sitting unassumingly at the table, he would likely have seen a faint smile emanate from the boy's youthful face. The family was now enjoying the fruits of young Donnie's labor, a scene repeated time and again at the Bowman household.

JOHNSON CITY AWARDED

A STATE NORMAL SCHOOL

Johnson City's most momentous event of 1911 was undoubtedly the opening of the East Tennessee State Normal School, now known as East Tennessee State University. During the 1908–09 legislative session, Tennessee lawmakers passed a bill that authorized the building of four "Normal Schools," three for white students and one for African American students, in carefully selected cities within the volunteer state.

The colleges were constructed for the explicit purpose of educating high school students on the standards (or norms) necessary to qualify them to serve as teachers in Tennessee high schools. The underlying aim was to eventually replace poorly prepared teachers with those who had better foundation training. After designating Nashville as the logical site for the black school, the legislature decided to award one city in each of the three natural divisions of the state—East Tennessee, Middle Tennessee and West Tennessee—a white school. These three geographic sections of the state are defined by the Tennessee River, a meandering body of water that was once named the Cherokee River. Its prolonged journey extends from the east side of Knoxville, south toward Chattanooga (dividing East and Middle Tennessee), into northern Alabama, west across the Mississippi border, north through Tennessee (separating Middle and West Tennessee) and finally flows into Kentucky as the largest tributary to empty into the Ohio River. The winners for a Normal School were Johnson City (East), Murfreesboro (Middle) and Memphis (West). The state government subsequently appropriated $1 million to be equally divided among the schools.

Among other East Tennessee cities actively vying for a school were Sweetwater, Dayton and Athens. The selection commission, led by Governor Malcolm R. Patterson, visited Johnson City in 1910 and scrutinized several potential property sites, including Carter Addition and Carnegie.

Washington County attendees included attorneys S.C. Williams and H.H. Carr, the *Comet* editor Cy Lyle, George F. Campbell, James A. Summers and others. The debate on behalf of Johnson City was discussed on the veranda of the former hotel of the Mountain Branch Soldiers' Home.

Cy Lyle cunningly offered his overt opinion of where the new school should be located in a February 15 newspaper article that contained both amusing and moving words:

In the beginning when God finished the universe, He rested from His labors in East Tennessee and found that He had an immense amount of mineral wealth left over after giving all portions of the world their quota. This He piled up around Johnson City and covered it with earth that the sluggard might "root hog or die." With lavish hand, He fringed the mounds with the giant timber and the clinging and creeping verdure that have called forth the admiration of the world. Standing upon the highest of these peaks, God looked over His handiwork, smiled at its rugged beauty and completeness and stepped easily into Heaven. It has been correctly stated that from the giant peaks you can tickle the feet of the angels, but a practical demonstration could not be made for the state board of education because the members had overlooked the essential feature of bringing their angels with them... There is more inspiration, determination, aspiration, and perspiration imbibed and required in climbing these hills than can be found at any other point in the state. Why shouldn't the normal be located in Johnson City?

After considering the pros and cons of each site, the state decided in favor of Carter Addition, located not far from the Soldiers' Home property that had been purchased a few years earlier. The school was to be built on a tract of 120 acres, situated on the southwestern outskirts of Johnson City, within view of a lofty chain of picturesque mountains a few miles away. The group was greatly influenced by the city's magnificent environment of "high elevation, beautiful scenery, ideal climate and pure freestone water." The *Comet* newspaper cunningly announced the thrilling news of the city's selection on December 2, 1909:

Johnson City gets the State Normal for East Tennessee. This result was reached by the State Board of Education Wednesday, noon after being in session since Monday morning. The joyful news reached Johnson City by wire immediately and every whistle in the city was dampened with steam and the lusty throated songsters conveyed the glad tidings to the community and the rejoicing was above Normal.

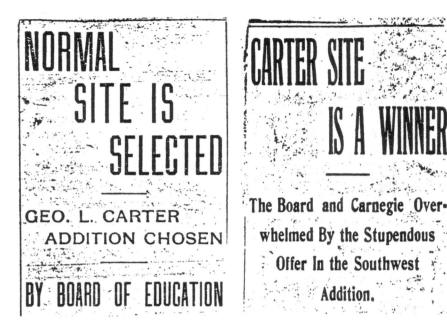

NORMAL SITE IS SELECTED
GEO. L. CARTER ADDITION CHOSEN
BY BOARD OF EDUCATION

CARTER SITE IS A WINNER
The Board and Carnegie Overwhelmed By the Stupendous Offer In the Southwest Addition.

Two newspaper article headlines from the *Comet* joyously proclaim that the chosen site for a Normal School will be the Carter Addition on the southwest side of town. *Courtesy of the Microfilm Library, East Tennessee State University*.

Recognizing the importance of the new facility, Washington County and Johnson City each appropriated $75,000 in bonds; Johnson City further agreed to supply the campus with "free water and lights." As promised, George L. Carter donated 120 acres of land valued at $60,000. Sidney J. Gilbreath, one of Tennessee's outstanding educators, was chosen as the first president. Among his impressive credentials were posts as public schoolteacher, county superintendent, college president, state superintendent, president of the Public School Officers Association, president of the State Teachers Association, professor at Peabody College for Teachers for four years and superintendent of the Chattanooga schools from 1903 to his selection for the East Tennessee Normal School in 1910. While the buildings were being constructed on campus, the newly appointed president occupied an office upstairs in the King Building at 225 East Main in downtown Johnson City. Two of his first priorities were to prepare the school's curricula and hire a qualified faculty. His selection of teachers was impressive; all were graduates of colleges and universities, including nearby Milligan and Tusculum Colleges.

Under direction of S.M. Beaumont Contracting Company of Knoxville, more than one hundred workmen, including carpenters, masons, electricians, molders, plumbers and others, hastened to erect the main campus structures—Gilbreath Hall, Carter Hall, the president's residence, a dining room and a heating plant—and have them ready for occupancy by the opening of the fall term.

The Normal School opened its doors for classes on September 5, 1911, with an enrollment of just twenty-nine students, a small number that would soon grow significantly. Each Normal School applicant was required to sign a pledge to teach in a public or private school in Tennessee for six years after graduation. In-state students were not charged tuition, but were assessed a $2 registration fee for each twelve-week term. Female students paid a $6 resident cost per term (there were no dormitories for men) and $1 for the six-week summer term. Out-of-state students were charged $12 per term and $6 for summer school. Students were promoted if they maintained a grade average of seventy-five, on the condition that they had a minimum of sixty in any course. An old newspaper advertisement for the Normal School showed the total cost of in-state fees to be just $150 a year, which included the cost of tuition, room and board and other expenses, excluding clothing.

The same law that established these Normal Schools provided for the training facilities to contract with local school districts in order to have students enrolled in Normal Schools serve as observation or "practice fields" for prospective teachers. In order to meet this requirement, the state and the schools contracted with the city allowed acceptance of high school students for the years 1911 through 1913 at an agreed-upon price of $4,000 a year. The school board was pleased with this arrangement because the cost of maintaining these students at Science Hill High School was $4,500. This agreement not only saved the city $500 per pupil, but it also exposed high school students to courses in agriculture, manual training, domestic science and commerce, subjects not offered in the high school curriculum. The contract was renewed in 1914 for an additional year. That same year, the Normal School decided to recruit its own students in grades one through twelve to provide this "practice field" for student teachers.

One of the conditions of the contract between the state and the city for having high school students enrolled in the Normal School was that trolley service would be provided to and from the Normal School by the Johnson City Traction Company. By July 1911, the trolley tracks had not been laid, prompting major concern for city officials. The July 13, 1911 issue of the *Comet* referred to the dilemma:

> *There is considerable discussion going the rounds in a sub-rosa sort of way as to the reason why the street car extension out to the Normal School is*

EAST TENNESSEE STATE UNIVERSITY

Created by the legislature in 1909, East Tennessee State Normal School was built on land given by George L. Carter. Official state flag was first raised at dedication ceremonies on October 10, 1911. The school became a teachers college in 1925, a college in 1943 and a university in 1963. The Quillen-Dishner College of Medicine opened in 1978. Original classroom building was named for first president Sidney G. Gilbreath.

A State of Tennessee historical marker offers a brief history of the school from its humble beginnings, when it was known as East Tennessee State Normal School. *Courtesy of the Bob Cox Collection.*

not underway as of yet. It will be remembered that a new franchise was granted to the Johnson City Traction Company by the Board of Aldermen some weeks ago provided work on the extension was begun within four months and the line to the Normal School completed in nine months. The four months have expired and no visible start appears except some crossings [cross-ties] piled at the CC&O crossing of Buffalo Street.

Mr. Amzi Smith, manager of the trolley system, vowed he would have the cars running by the time the school opened. The Traction Company ultimately made good on its promise by scheduling crews of tracklayers and stringers for thirteen-hour workdays. The *Comet* later acknowledged its astonishment that the streetcar facilities to the newly built school were completed during July, August and September, in time for opening day, admitting that it was "the quickest display of engineering seen anywhere in the South."

The dedication of East Tennessee's new Normal School took place in the school's main auditorium on October 10, 1911, eight days after the opening of the first session. The dedicatory exercises were as follows:

> *Rev. L.B. Stivers, pastor of the Central Baptist Church, read a scripture lesson; Dr. Dayton A. Dobbs, pastor of the Watauga Avenue Presbyterian Church, delivered the dedicatory prayer; Judge E.B. Hensley of Washington County and Mayor W.A. Dickinson and Superintendent J.L. Brooks of Johnson City spoke briefly on securing the location of the school; State Superintendent J.W. Brister delivered an address on "Our Normal Schools: Their Aims and Purposes;" Mrs. Elizabeth Cratcer, President of the Woman's Relief Corps, presented a flag to the school; President S.G. Gilbreath replied with an address of acceptance; ex-Governor John I. Cox, who had championed the senate bill establishing the state normal system; and Honorable A.A. [Alf] Taylor, made short addresses; Dr. P.P. Claxton, U.S. Commissioner of Education and a pioneer crusader in Tennessee for an improved public school system, including the establishment of state normal schools, spoke on the purpose of the school and gave his vision of its progress through the future years; and Honorable Samuel H. Thompson, member of the State Board, spoke on "East Tennessee: An Opportunity."*
>
> *At the conclusion of the program in the assembly hall, the audience was dismissed to the grounds, where the flag, presented by the Woman's Relief Corps, was raised. The dedicatory exercises closed with a luncheon given in the new dining hall in honor of guests of the school.*

By 1915, the beautiful campus had expanded, with buildings valued at over $208,000 and a student enrollment of 1,000. The Normal School was deemed "the heart of the public school system." It offered two distinct curriculums—an academic one of four years and a normal one requiring two additional years of study. The school drew immediate attention, and within three years, it had an enrollment of 2,933. Further evidence of the school's worth was noted when the University of Tennessee announced that graduates of the state Normal School would be accepted at the Knoxville campus and awarded bachelor's degrees from the institution upon successful completion of two years additional study there. In 1928, a high school, known

The Normal School as it looked thirty-six years later in 1947. By this time, the name had been changed to East Tennessee State College. *Courtesy of Doris Anderson (taken from 1947 East Tennessee State College Annual,* The Buccaneer*).*

as the Training School and later renamed University High, was erected on the college campus at a cost of approximately $225,000. Another significant milestone for the institution occurred in 1963, when East Tennessee State College became East Tennessee State University. The year 1974 brought about a further major happening—the formation of the James H. Quillen College of Medicine.

The university's impressive evolution from a modest beginning in 1911 to the present can best be summarized by a statement on its website:

> *East Tennessee State University opened its doors in 1911 to prepare teachers for the region's public schools and has been serving the Northeast Tennessee community ever since. Today, ETSU serves the region's business community, P-12 and postsecondary educational systems, government agencies, health care systems, and general public. We are committed to service that strengthens our region and, in turn, enriches our students, faculty, and staff.*

HARRISON FAMILY
BLESSED WITH A BAKER'S
DOZEN OF BOYS

An event that took place in early May 1955 near Johnson City drew attention in newspapers all over the country. The story unfolded in two parts over the next four years. Emory and Thelma Harrison, of Washington County, had the atypical distinction of having thirteen sons and no daughters. It was believed that they were the largest all-male-child family in the country at the time.

The Harrison family ranged in age from twenty-one-year-old Guy to three-week-old Ivan. The others were Foy, Gordon, David, Richard, John, Sam, Bob, Haskel, Ray, George and Carmel. Money-poor all his life, the elder Harrison said that his children never caused him and his wife a speck of trouble, and he knew the reason why:

> It's the way we raise them. We raise them to obey us, never to bother anybody and never pick up anything that belonged to anybody else. If they need a spanking, they get it, but they don't need it often. Each has chores to do. One feeds the hogs corn; one feeds them slops; one does the milking; some dry the dishes; some cut wood; and others carry it in.

Emory further explained that all the boys helped each other. He said that the older boys were just as crazy about a new baby as he and his wife were. He went on to say:

> There never was a child born but what there was a bite of food made to fill its mouth with, but there have been fathers and mothers too trifling to fill a child's mouth. When we had one child, we just lived. When we had six children, we lived. Now we have thirteen and we're still living.

The Emory and Thelma Harrison family pose barefoot after arriving in New York City by train. *Newspaper clipping from the* Atlanta Journal, *May 5, 1955.*

The tall, lanky farmer was forced to quit school in the fourth grade to work on the family farm. Others described him as being a man of natural dignity, possessing a rich vein of homespun humor. A large family was normal fare for the Harrisons. His wife had fifteen siblings. His grandfather, whom he described as a religious man, had twenty-seven children from three wives and rode a red mule to church every Sunday until he was eighty-five years old.

A noteworthy event occurred in the Harrison home in May 1955. Mrs. Harrison was selected "Honor Mother of the Year" by an interfaith movement in New York City for her exemplary life as wife, mother and neighbor. She was invited to visit the Big Apple to accept her prestigious and well-earned award. Since she and her husband could not leave their family behind, the expense of fifteen people traveling to Manhattan was far beyond their financial capability. The journey initially appeared to be in doubt, but the problem was quickly resolved when a clothing firm graciously paid for all of them to go to New York. Leaving the uncomplicated rural life of Washington County to visit the bustling bright lights and frantic crowds of the teeming big city was an experience they would not soon forget.

Train tickets were purchased and delivered to them to handle their travel needs. Arriving at the Southern Depot near Fountain Square in downtown Johnson City, the family boarded Southern Railway's "The Tennessean" for their approximate 630-mile excursion by rail to New York City. Over the next four days, the now-famous family attended the award ceremony to witness the bestowal of the title of "Honor Mother of the Year" upon Mrs. Harrison. To their pleasurable surprise, they were invited to appear on NBC's network television show *On Your Account*, sponsored by Proctor and Gamble. Eddie Elbert, who would later be known as Oliver Douglas

Harrison Family Blessed with a Baker's Dozen of Boys

on another television program, *Green Acres*, emceed the program. Selected players answered questions to win money for charity or a deserving individual. The Harrisons were certainly deserving and subsequently were awarded an astonishing $3,200 worth of prizes on the show—a hefty amount in 1955.

At the end of the four days, the glitter of Manhattan started to tarnish and the weary and homesick clan was ready to make the return trip by rail to their plaintive farmstead near the Tennessee mountains. Emory explained their desire to come home best when he proclaimed, "It's corn plantin' time." Back home, he was asked numerous questions from inquisitive folks who read about the award ceremony and the Harrisons' journey to New York. Most of the inquiries related to what it was like raising such a large family of boys and no girls. The father emphatically responded that he did not see why poverty should cause juvenile delinquency in his family members.

The Emory Harrison family story does not end with May 1955. Almost four years later, on April 28, 1959, the stork, who by then could find his way to the Harrison household blindfolded and was likely getting weary of making so many deliveries there, made a fourteenth visit, bringing, not another boy, but a beautiful little girl. She was named Barbara Ann and had the likely distinction of being the only girl in the country with thirteen brothers.

JOHN ROBINSON CIRCUS'S
EXHILARATING ANNUAL
TREK TO CITY

A much-anticipated event routinely occurred in Johnson City from the early 1900s to the early 1930s, when the John F. Robinson Circus rolled into town on the railroad, bringing with it much excitement and high expectations for area residents.

Governor Harry F. Byrd of Virginia, who attended the show at Richmond in August 1928 just prior to its arrival in Johnson City, hosted six hundred orphan children from several city institutions and summarily wrote the following letter to Sam B. Dill, the circus's general manager, commenting on his reaction to seeing a performance. The correspondence displays the public official's opinion of the worth of the annual event:

> *Gentleman. It affords me pleasure to testify to the high merits of your capital exhibition, as presented in this city yesterday at both afternoon and night performances. Your show was both recreational and educational and I am pleased to learn was enjoyed by capacity audiences. From the cages of the animals to the big tent, your exhibition was complete with thrills and daring. Your acrobatic artists and clowns were both of a high type, as were also your animal trainers and horses. Taken as a whole, you presented a clean and most enjoyable entertainment and one, which I have no hesitancy in recommending highly to the public. With best wishes, Harry Byrd, Governor of Virginia.*

Several *Johnson City Chronicle and Staff-News* newspapers from that era offer particulars about the gala happening. During the October 14, 1930 stopover, a "Grand Free $30,000 Street Parade" was conducted from downtown Fountain Square to Keystone Field near Tannery Knob. The well-attended procession included a "Fife and Drum Corps, Chime of Bells, 50 Cars and

Johnson City, Thursday, August 18th

This page: John Robinson Circus newspaper advertisements from the August 14, 1927 *Johnson City Staff News. Courtesy of the Microfilm Library, East Tennessee State University.*

John Robinson Circus's Exhilarating Annual Trek to City

Guided Dens, 29 Tableau Cars, 12 Traps, Two Herds of Elephants, 300 Thoroughbred Horses, 50 Miniature Ponies and a Steam Calliope Drawn by 40 Ponies and Driven by One Man."

The elephants originally belonged to the Carl Hagenback Circus's herd of $40,000 performing five-toed pachyderms. At the impressive Water Carnival in Germany every year, Hagenback, known worldwide for its animal training abilities, always furnished the festival's main feature. It was said that this renowned amusement caterer was to the old world what John Robinson, heralded as the king of showmen, was to the new. John purchased his four highly trained elephants from Hagenback, and the act became a major feature of the Robinson show as it journeyed across America.

An advertisement from that year revealed one hundred new and novel circus acts, plus an additional one hundred rare and costly animals. It further showed four circuses and three menageries performing on two stages and a Roman Hippodrome (oval horse track). The cast was composed of five hundred men, women and horses. Another production, titled King Solomon and the Queen of Sheba, featured "an impressive and eminently moral and mind-elevating pageantic and scenic spectacle, with its enchanting ballets, magnificent scenery and gorgeous costumes." The cast included one hundred beautiful ballet girls.

An itemized listing of the various acts included a drove of camels, a whole family of twenty lions, four royal Bengal tigers, six polar bears, a school of sea lions, a den of six hyenas, a pair of elands (antelopes), a pair of horned horses, every known species of antelope, ten male bareback riders, ten female riders, fifty aerial acts, ten wire acts, a troupe of trained ponies, twenty female equestrians, a two-foot-tall Philippine Cow and a baby sea lion. Several races were held, as well—male hippodrome, monkey, elephant, camel, man against horses, two-horse tandem, high-jumping horses, two- and four-horse chariot and two- and four-horse standing.

The local *Johnson City Chronicle and Staff News* held a unique contest, offering twelve free tickets. Contained in each of the ads for the carnival was part of a picture of a circus animal and its trainer. The rules said to simply cut all the parts from the ads and paste them on a sheet of paper with the person's name and address. The paper cautioned that neatness was a factor in choosing a winner. The paper was then to be mailed to the circus contest editor of the paper. Winners were announced in the newspaper the day before the show, and several reserved-seat tickets were awarded under first-, second-, third- and fourth-place categories.

The railroads took advantage of the event by offering reduced fares for folks to ride the train from distant areas. An estimated two thousand people

A circus parade down Walnut Street near the site of Model Mill Company, just off of Walnut Street. *Courtesy of the Archives of Appalachia, East Tennessee State University.*

The circus tent of the John Robinson Circus, located between Main and Market Streets near the city's main fire station. *Courtesy of the Archives of Appalachia, East Tennessee State University.*

rode to Johnson City on the special circus excursions conducted by the Carolina, Clinchfield and Ohio and the East Tennessee and Western North Carolina railroads on Thursday. The CC&O excursion left Alta Pass, North Carolina, at 8:00 a.m. and arrived in Johnson City at 10:50 a.m. The fare was $1.50, with corresponding low rates from other stations. The ET&WNC train left Boone, North Carolina, at 5:50 a.m. and arrived in Johnson City at 10:25 a.m. A special train left Johnson City on the return trip at 5:00 p.m., forty-five minutes after the conclusion of the afternoon show, and reached Boone at 9:30 p.m. The round-trip fare from Boone was $2.40, with low rates prevailing from the other stations. Visitors had the option of remaining overnight in Johnson City if they did not wish to return on the special train; they could instead hop on the regular one on Friday.

About seventy-five "newsies," newspaper carriers as they were known then, of the *Johnson City Chronicle and Staff-News* were complimentary guests of the circus at the big show on Keystone Field Thursday night. Jess N. Bailey, then circulation manager of the combined carrier forces of the two local papers, arranged for carriers of the *Chronicle and Staff-News* from both Elizabethton and Erwin to attend the circus as a group. Long before the time set for leaving, the "newsies" gathered in front of the Appalachian Publishers building at West Main and Boone, all dressed up "to see the elephants and monkeys, lions and tigers, and to feed peanuts to Jumbo and drink pink lemonade." Those having *Staff-News* routes had to rush through their afternoon deliveries to get home, dress for the occasion and arrive on time at West Main. The circus's munificence further allowed the carriers to bring their younger brothers with them, also at no charge.

Just as fast as it arrived, the "Biggest Show on Earth" concluded its performances, pulled up stakes and moved on to another city to bring excitement and joy to the next municipality on its planned timetable. Johnson Citians had to wait a year for its return.

COLLECTOR JIM WELSH

DESIRED NEW JOHNSON CITY

SONGS

The casual mention of the name Jim Walsh would likely evoke little or no response from Johnson Citians, young or old, compared to the likes of former congressman B. Carroll Reece; Tennessee governors Bob and Alf Taylor; newspaper publisher Carl Jones; Heisman trophy winner and legendary football coach Steve Spurrier; author of the wartime novel *Bridge to the Sun* Gwen Terasaki; Major League Baseball player Ferrell Bowman; and others.

Walsh's name may not register on the Richter scale of Johnson City's "Who's Who," but based on his mammoth contributions to vintage music, he justly deserves his "place in the sun." He was christened Ulysses James Walsh upon birth in 1903. His father, an avid admirer of General Ulysses S. Grant, named his son after the Union officer, causing a bit of a rift with Southern Civil War sympathizers. That concern later forced him to drop all references to the former president, and he became known as Jim Walsh.

The future record collector and magazine editor began his career as a journalist with several newspapers, including the *Knoxville News-Sentinel*. He once mentioned that his first big break came in 1934, when he became affiliated with the *Johnson City Press*, remaining with them until 1942. In his new position, he served as chief reporter, editorial writer, feature writer and columnist. In 1943, he returned to his home state of Virginia to work as a staff writer for the *Roanoke World-News*. He was also affiliated in Roanoke with WSLS-Radio-TV and, beginning in June 1964, was a staff writer for the *Roanoke Times*.

During Walsh's last four years of employment with the *Johnson City Press*, he developed a ravenous appetite for old records, eventually amassing an astonishing collection of forty thousand 78 rpm records and five hundred Edison cylinders. Conspicuously absent from his impressive compilation of numerous genres were classical records. Walsh not only accumulated discs, but he also researched songs and artists so thoroughly that he likely became the preeminent authority of such music in American history. This accolade, in turn, led him to begin hosting a program appropriately named *Wax Works* over local radio station WJHL. Even though Jim eventually moved from the mountainous Johnson City region, he later acknowledged that he liked living there better than anywhere else he had resided. He was duly impressed by the musical heritage of the area, but in a 1950 newspaper article he lamented the fact that no new songs had been written about the city in a long time:

> *Probably no state in the union has had more songs written about it than Tennessee. Included is "Carry Me Back to Tennessee," which was published 97 years ago in 1853....Now that "Chattanooga Shoeshine Boy" has gone over the hill, seems it's time for some up and coming songwriter to do a number about Johnson City. As a former resident of the metropolis of Washington County who still likes it better than any place that I have ever lived, I resent the fact that there hasn't been, to my knowledge, a new song about Johnson City in years. It was not always so. During the late 1920s and early 1930s, a surprisingly large number of tunes were recorded about Johnson City and most of them were sung and played by local musicians.*
>
> *Both Johnson City and Bristol were the centers in those days for their recording of that type of music summed up in the word "hillbilly." Scouts for the big phonograph companies, making periodic expeditions into the South, would set up recording equipment and East Tennessee musicians would flock in. But what I'm primarily concerned with right now is the lack of present-day songs about Johnson City. Pears to me like the tune twisters ain't doing right by my famous old hometown. If somebody'll write a new song about Johnson City and get it recorded. I'll promise to buy a copy of the record.*

Walsh mentioned another radio show that he hosted, impertinently titled *The Old Wreck with the Old Records*, that featured his massive collection of time-honored phonograph records. He made it a point to obtain a copy of every new record that was issued and met his interest, especially those that had a Tennessee flavor associated with them. One of his favorite songs was Clarence Greene's "Johnson City Blues," recorded at the 1928 Johnson City Sessions. Walsh recalled meeting Greene a couple of times. Another song the record collector noted was "Johnson City Rag," recorded at the 1929 Johnson City Sessions by the Roane County Ramblers. Fiddlin' Charlie Bowman made a contribution to his hometown by writing "East Tennessee

Blues," an instrumental ditty recorded by Al Hopkins and His Buckle Busters (a.k.a., The Hill Billies) on jointly owned Brunswick and Vocalion Records. One unusual local song was titled "Pot Licker Blues," performed by a black mouth harp musician, El Watson and Charles Johnson for Victor Records during the 1928 Bristol Sessions. The term "Pot Liquor" referred to the black section of Johnson City that once spread west from Carver Park on West Watauga Avenue.

Walsh further commented on musicians Lester Macfarland and Robert Gardner, who recorded "Chattanooga Blues." Some of the words of that song are nearly identical with those of "Johnson City Blues." In 1913, Irving Berlin came through with a humorous song, "Down in Chattanooga." Allegedly, the singer had difficulty pronouncing the name of the city and called it "Chattahooga." Perhaps the best-known song carrying that city's name in the title is the 1941 "Chattanooga Choo-Choo."

Nashville had its fair share of songs with "Come On to Nashville, Tennessee," "Nashville Nightingale," "The Nashville Blues" and "Nashville Skyline Rag," among others. Memphis sported what was probably Tennessee's most famous song, "The Memphis Blues" (1912), written by black composer W.C. Hand. Other songs were "I'm Goin' Back to Memphis, Tennessee," "Beale Street Blues" and "Beale Street Mama."

Additional records from Walsh's collection included one of Tennessee's biggest song hits, "The Girl I Loved in Sunny Tennessee," which came out in 1899; "Tennessee Waltz," one of the state songs; "There's a Warm Spot in My Heart for Tennessee"; Tennessee Moon"; "Celebrating Day in Tennessee"; "Tennessee, I Hear You Calling Me"; "My Sunny Tennessee"; "Down Among the Sleepy Hills of Tennessee"; "Tennessee Stud"; and "Mother Me, Tennessee." In 1967, another state song and the University of Tennessee's fight song, "Rocky Top," would be introduced to the music world.

Walsh made an observation that if the true old English language, as distinct from the American language, exists anywhere in America, it lives in the mountainous regions of Appalachia, in such towns as Johnson City. The preservation of the old, pure forms of speech has been dependent upon great mountain barriers. Examinations of the mountain ballads reveal that they tend to be sung much in the same manner as those of Elizabethan England. When the mountain people saw that the East Coast of America was becoming crowded, they pushed farther west until they crossed the Appalachian Mountains. They brought with them the songs and tales to which they had been accustomed in England. Some individuals tend to show contempt to "hillbilly" music, labeling it uneducated, uncouth and corny, but it should be remembered that the roots of the music are actually as pure and as representative of the people of a former time as one of Beethoven's great symphonies is representative of his era. This mountain music has lived longer than any other musical form that has come to America, and it continues to do so with each generation of old-time music lovers.

In the fall of 1960, Walsh was responsible for local musician, vaudeville performer and future member of the North American Fiddlers Hall of Fame, Fiddlin' Charlie Bowman, gaining a bit of notoriety toward the waning years of the fiddler's career. The journalist sent him a "penny postcard" on September 28, responding to a letter sent to him by Charlie. By this time, old-time or hillbilly music was passing off the scene and soon would be replaced by a new genre, rock and roll music, which would be more appealing to the youthful generation. Although working then at WSLS in Roanoke, Virginia, it appeared that Walsh still maintained some connection with the *Johnson City Press* because he agreed to write an article about Charlie's career and submit it to the newspaper. On the postcard, he mentioned that he was going to write another article for the *Press* about his visit to Thomas A. Edison's laboratory at West Orange, New Jersey, where he had been master of ceremonies.

While it is not known if Walsh ever wrote the newspaper article he promised, it is acknowledged that he featured Charlie in the October 1960 edition of *Hobbies Magazine*, as part of an ongoing section devoted to "Favorite Pioneer Recording Artists," often written in installments such as the one depicting Vernon Dalhart. Since Walsh knew the country crooner, he included photos of Charlie playing his fiddle; his two daughters, Jennie and Pauline holding instruments; and banjoist Jack Reedy at a folk music festival at White Top Mountain, Virginia, in the Appalachian Mountains. The record collector had this to say about the series:

> Hobbies' *decision to publish articles now and then for collectors of old-time "popular" records is particularly gratifying to me since I was more or less the pioneer prophet of this now well-established cult.*

Once, when asked to name the most outstanding pioneer recording artists of all time, the record expert offered fifteen names: Billy Murray, Henry Burr, Ada Jones, Len Spencer, Arthur Collins, Byron G. Harlan, Harry Macdonough, Albert Campbell, Frank C. Stanley, Steve Porter, Billy Golden, S.H. Dudley, Dan W. Quinn, William F. Hooley and Cal Stewart (known as Uncle Josh). Walsh knew the recordings of these artists better than any other writer.

Jim Walsh's voluminous record and document collection was donated in installments to the nation's Library of Congress between 1965 and 1987.

Collector Jim Welsh Desired New Johnson City Songs

OCTOBER *Hobbies* 1960

The Magazine For Collectors

PRESIDENTIAL CAMPAIGN COTTON
(See Page 29)

The October 30, 1960 front cover of *Hobbies Magazine*, edited by James Walsh. *Courtesy of the Charlie Bowman Collection*.

The compilation was organized into seven categories: Correspondence/ Research Files, Writings, Radio Scripts, Ephemera, Photographs, Oversize Materials and Volumes. Walsh's final years were spent in a nursing home in Roanoke, Virginia, until his passing on April 8, 1987. While his life ended that day, his legacy lives on because of his unselfish efforts to preserve his work at the nation's library. He was posthumously awarded the first Lifetime Achievement Award given by the Association for Recorded Sound Collections (ARSC) in 1991. Johnson Citians can certainly be proud of Jim Walsh.

RESIDENT'S FIRST
AUTOMOBILE RIDE WAS IN
AN AMBULANCE

Fuller Barnes had a unique distinction: his first ride in a motor vehicle occurred while being transported by ambulance to a Johnson City hospital. In 1947, the seventy-two-year-old resident shared from his hospital bed his lingering memories of life in Johnson City around the turn of the twentieth century.

Fuller and his wife, Mary, were married in 1895 in Gray Station, Tennessee, and lived out their lives in a single-story, crude wood house situated along Buffalo Ridge Road (later renamed Hales Chapel Road). Across the road from their log house was a steep hill containing the cemetery of the original Buffalo Ridge Baptist Church, reported to be the oldest house of worship in Tennessee. Fuller and Mary made a living off their land. In addition, Fuller served as a substitute mail carrier and delivered the county mail by horseback.

In 1907, at age thirty-two, Fuller became the victim of an unfortunate accident while performing chores on his farm, resulting in his becoming an invalid for the remainder of his life. He had gone to the barn to feed his cows a mixture of hay and corn fodder. Soon after climbing into the upper level, he noticed that someone had inadvertently moved his ladder, apparently unaware that he was up there. Not seeing anyone around to put his ladder back, he impatiently threw out a bundle of hay and fodder onto the ground and unwisely jumped on it, thinking it was thick enough to cushion his fall. He was wrong. The impact severely injured the vertebrae in his back. Even the best surgeons of the early 1900s were not medically equipped to repair the damage that he sustained. Numerous wagon trips to chiropractors in nearby Fall Branch and Johnson City offered him little relief, and he was left incapacitated for the duration of his life. Over the next forty years, Fuller rarely left the confines of his rustic country dwelling, and he experienced

The Barnes family home in Gray, Tennessee. Fuller and Mary are on the porch at the far left. *Courtesy of the Charlie Bowman Collection.*

firsthand a familiar saying from American playwright John Howard Paine, "Be it ever so humble, there's no place like home."

In 1947, Barnes was transported a short distance by ambulance to Budd Clinic and Hospital at 217 East Watauga Avenue in Johnson City for a brief hospital stay and treatment of varicose veins. In spite of his prolonged convalescence, this was his first bed-confining illness in all those years. Fuller also confessed to friends that this twelve-mile ambulance ride to the big city was his first ride in an automobile. Additionally, it was the farthest he had ventured from home since his injury in 1907. Regrettably, he was unable to tour the city and observe firsthand the changes that had taken place. However, several family members explored the town and related to him how much it had changed. Streets had not been paved when he visited there prior to 1907. The Washington County inhabitant felt that very little of value had been gained in the world between 1900 and 1947, a time period that included two horrific world wars and a lingering depression. Fuller was not impressed with how the area had changed during those forty-seven years. He longed for the peaceful and carefree 1900s lifestyle that he once enjoyed so much. He

The BEE HIVE

THE COFFEE POT ASSUMES A NEW PLACE IN YOUR ESTIMATION WHEN IT BREWS THE DELICIOUS CHASE & SANBORN'S HIGH GRADE COFFEE

For good, things to eat and for the best COFFEE and TEAS

Fine Candies Are a Specialty

WARD & FRIBERG

The Bee Hive was a general department store that once operated in downtown Johnson City, near Fountain Square, around the turn of the century. From the *Comet*, January 28, 1904. *Courtesy of the Microfilm Library, East Tennessee State University.*

commented that about all mankind had learned during that time was how to round highway curves at speeds of sixty miles an hour, work faster at every undertaking and become consumed by the ever-constant pursuit of money. He believed that man's ultimate payback for this unfortunate lifestyle was dying at an early age without achieving his long-sought-after hefty goals.

The memory-laden Fuller reminisced about the relaxed days of growing up in the beautiful mountains and valleys surrounding Johnson City. He recalls when it was a thriving town of horses, buggies, streetcars, automobiles and trains; when great strides in manufacturing and mercantile fields had been accomplished. Streets then were muddy and sidewalks, if any were present, usually consisted of wooden planks. Barnes fondly recalled two landmark businesses in downtown Johnson City: the New York Racket and the Bee Hive. Proprietors P.M. Ward and C.D. Friberg owned the latter business, a large department store located on Main Street in the heart of the business district. Opened in 1890, the company offered dry goods, millinery, ladies' ready-to-wear, shoes, gent's furnishings, groceries, hardware, stationery, wallpaper, mattings, sundries and prescription drugs. The former resident also recalled two photographic businesses during that colorful era—Cargille Studios was located in Johnson City, and Keene Studio operated from Jonesboro.

Barnes's usual mode of transportation in those days was astride a horse. During visits to the inner city, he frequently stopped at the Faw spring located at the corner of Roan and Market Streets to fetch a drink of cool, refreshing water, rest and have lunch. This popular "water hole" would later become the site of Johnson City's ten-story "skyscraper," the John Sevier Hotel. When told of the big hotel, Fuller eagerly wanted to know if the old spring was still useful in supplying a portion of the water supply to the upstate area's leading hostelry. Barnes recalled when Johnson City's young mayor, Davie A. Vines, served between 1904 and 1906. The attorney led a long, uninterrupted public life, which later included serving as a circuit court judge. Fuller further remembered when Tennessee's democratic governor, John Isaac Cox from neighboring Sullivan County, was elevated to Speaker of the state senate upon the resignation of James B. Frazier after Frazier was appointed United State senator in 1905. Fuller told of the presidency being filled in 1901 by the "aggressive cowboy," Teddy Roosevelt, who became the nation's leader after the assassination of President William McKinley. Barnes cast his first ballot in 1896 for McKinley. He credited his GOP political faith to his father, David Barnes, who served in the Union army during the Civil War.

Barnes said that recreational activities were limited in his days. He farmed the very ground that his father had tilled before him. Pleasure time away from the grime of farm work included the hunting of such small game as rabbits and squirrels. The old-timer lamented that such animals were much scarcer now. Another source of merriment was playing music. He played fiddle with his wife's three brothers, Charlie, Walter and Argil Bowman. Fuller fondly recalled when he and the Bowman brothers entertained locals at the old Barton School near Asbury.

Fuller's religious faith was aligned with Mount Zion in the Gray Station community. He recalls attending the camp meetings at Sulphur Springs in the "old days," when whole families would come in wagons. Camp meetings of that time were a cherished religious tradition and a link with the pioneer forebears. The influence of those get-togethers went beyond the limits of the campgrounds. Rural women prepared and served the best food grown right on their farms.

Sadly, Fuller Barnes passed away in Gray Station on August 10, 1951. His loyal wife of fifty-six years joined him seven years later on August 15, 1958. Fuller Barnes rendered the city a big service by making a valuable withdrawal from his memory bank of some cherished recollections of early Johnson City.

BIBLIOGRAPHY

A Brief History of a Beautiful, Mountainous Land

McGee, G.R. *A History of Tennessee from 1663 to 1905*. New York: American Book Company, 1899.

Parks, Joseph, and Stanley Flomsbee. *The Story of Tennessee*. Norman, OK: Harlow Publishing Corporation, 1952/1973.

Peterson, Thomas. *Historical Sketches of the Holston Valleys*. Kingsport, TN: Kingsport Press, 1926.

Piedmont Directory Company. *Johnson City Directory*. 1911.

Ramsey, J.G.M. *The Annals of Tennessee to the End of the Eighteenth Century*. Philadelphia: J.B. Lippincott and Company, 1860.

Science Hill High School. *The Wataugan*. 1939.

Smith, J. Gray. *A Brief Historical, Statistical and Descriptive Review of East Tennessee, United State of America*. Spartanburg, SC: The Reprint Company, 1842/1974.

Weaver, Clarence E. *Illustrated Johnson City Tennessee*. Central Publishing Company, 1915.

Williams, Samuel Cole. *History of Johnson City and Its Environs*. Johnson City, TN: The Watauga Press, 1940.

Henry Johnson: Johnson City's Unpretentious Founder

Goodspeed's History of Tennessee from the Earliest Time to the Present. Chicago: The Goodspeed Publishing Company, 1887.

BIBLIOGRAPHY

Johnson City Chronicle, May 21, 1922.
Johnson City Press, May 25, 1969.
Johnson City Staff-News, September 21, 1926.
Jonesborough Herald and Tribune, March 26, 1874.
Watauga Association of Genealogists, Upper East Tennessee. *History of Washington County Tennessee.* 1988.
Williams, Samuel Cole. *History of Johnson City and Its Environs.* Johnson City, TN: The Watauga Press, 1940.

A DEBATING SOCIETY BECAME SCIENCE HILL HIGH SCHOOL

Johnson City Comet, 1884.
McCown, Mary Hardin. "Science Hill Male and Female Institute, 1867–1967." Address given at the centennial celebration of Science Hill High School, October 30, 1967.
The Wataugan, 1939.

WERE THE TAYLOR BROTHERS FIDDLERS OR VIOLINISTS?

Cox, Bob L. *Fiddlin' Charlie Bowman.* Knoxville: The University of Tennessee Press, 2007.
McGee, G.R. *A History of Tennessee from 1663 to 1905.* New York: American Book Company, 1899.
Zimmerman, Peter Coats. *Tennessee Music, Its People and Places.* San Francisco: Miller Freeman Books, 1998.

JOHNSON CITY'S LOVE AFFAIR WITH THE COUNTY FAIR

Johnson City Comet, October 3, 1901.
Johnson City Staff-News, August 19, 1928; September 9, 1928; October 16, 1928; October 17, 1928.

BUSINESSES FLOURISHED AT THE TURN OF THE CENTURY

Johnson City Comet, July 16, 1903.

BIBLIOGRAPHY

Piedmont Directory Company. Archives of Appalachia, East Tennessee State University. 1909.

EVOLUTION OF JOHNSON'S DEPOT INTO A MULTI-RAILROAD TOWN

Daniels, Ophelia Cope. "The Formative Years of Johnson City, Tennessee, 1885–1890, A Social History." Thesis, Tennessee Agricultural and Industrial State College, 1947.

Johnson City Press-Chronicle, September 13, 1984.

Lewis, J.O. *Johnson City, Tennessee.* Johnson City, TN: The Overmountain Press, 1989. Original compiled in 1909 by J.O. Lewis, secretary of the Commercial Club.

Scheer, Julian, and Lee Kolbe. *Tweetsie—The Blue Ridge Stemwinder.* Johnson City, TN: The Overmountain Press, 1958/1991.

The Wataugan. Science Hill High School annual, 1939.

Weaver, Clarence E. *Illustrated Johnson City Tennessee.* Central Publishing Company, 1915.

THE PRODIGAL "LADY OF THE FOUNTAIN" COMES HOME

E-mail correspondence from the Zollicoffer family.

Johnson City Press, March 7, 2005; April 4, 2005; October 15, 2007.

Johnson City Press-Chronicle: October 31, 1971; September 21, 1983; May 29, 1989.

THE NEW "SOLDIERS' HOME" WAS A MOMENTOUS EVENT

Johnson City Comet, circa 1901.

CLARENCE GREENE'S 1928 "JOHNSON CITY BLUES"

Answers.com. s.v. "Byrd Moore." http://www.answers.com/Byrd%20Moore.

Greene, Clarence Howard. Interview by Bob Cox and Alan Bridwell, February 5, 2008, and subsequent follow-up written correspondence.

Bibliography

Haymes, "Mississippi" Max. "Got the Blues for Chattanooga." Earlyblues.com. http://www.earlyblues.com/Got%20The%20Blues% 20For%20Chattanooga.htm.

Wolfe, Dr. Charles. Notes from a seminar lecture. Birthplace of Country Music Alliance, Bristol, Tennessee. April 2004.

The Bizarre Account of an Elephant Hanging

Johnson City Press-Chronicle, March 31, 1987; June 10, 1987; April 19, 1990; July 10, 1992.

Price, Charles Edwin. *The Day They Hung The Elephant.* Johnson City: The Overmountain Press, 1992.

Schroeder, Joan Vannorsdall. "There's A Skeleton In A Trainyard In East Tennessee." Blue Ridge Country. www.blueridgecountry.com.

The Dreadful Newspaper Headline: "Our Bob Is Dead"

Allison, Judge John. *Notable Men of Tennessee.* Atlanta: Southern Historical Association, 1905.

Augsburg, Paul Deresco. *Bob and Alf Taylor—Their Lives and Lectures.* Morristown, TN: Morristown Book Company, Inc., 1925.

Cox, Joyce, and W. Eugene. *History of Washington County Tennessee.* Johnson City, TN: The Overmountain Press, 2001.

Johnson City Comet, undated; April 4, 1912.

Senate Proceedings of February 8, 1913. *Robert Love Taylor Memorial Address.* Washington: The Joint Proceedings on Printing, 1912.

Taylor, Bob. *Lectures and Best Literary Productions of Bob Taylor.* Nashville, TN: The Bob Taylor Publishing Company, 1912.

Taylor Brothers (James P., Alf A and Hugh L.). *Life and Career of Senator Robert Love Taylor (Our Bob).* Nashville: The Bob Taylor Publishing Company, 1913.

July Fourth Celebrations Were Once Big Happenings

Johnson City Press-Chronicle, May 25, 1969.

Confessions of a Youthful, Gravel-Flipping Sharpshooter

Cox, Bob. *Bowman Family Newsletter*, April 2002.
Johnson City Press-Chronicle, June 10, 1979.

Johnson City Awarded a State Normal School

Burleson, David Sinclair. *History of the East Tennessee State College*. Johnson City: East Tennessee State College, 1947.
ETSU Website. "Serving the Region...Preserving the Past and Shaping the Future." http://www.etsu.edu/etsu/region.asp.
Johnson City Comet, December 2, 1909; October 21, 1909 (reprinted from the *Nashville American*); October 15, 1909.
Parks, Joseph, and Stanley Flomsbee. *The Story of Tennessee*. Norman, OK: Harlow Publishing Corporation, 1952/1973.
Stahl, Ray. *A Beacon to Health Care—The Story of The Johnson City Medical Center Hospital*, Johnson City, TN: Printing Concepts, Inc., 1989.
Van West, Carroll. *Tennessee Encyclopedia of History & Culture*. Knoxville: The University of Tennessee Press, 2002. Electronic edition, Knoxville Historical Society.
Weaver, Clarence E. *Illustrated Johnson City Tennessee*. Central Publishing Company, 1915.
Williams, Samuel Cole. *History of Johnson City and Its Environs*. Johnson City, TN: The Watauga Press, 1940.

Harrison Family Blessed with a Baker's Dozen of Boys

Atlanta Journal, May 5, 1955.
Johnson City Press-Chronicle, May 7, 1959.

John Robinson Circus's Exhilarating Annual Trek to City

Johnson City Comet, October 14, 1902.
Johnson City Staff-News, August 14, 1927; August 19, 1927.

BIBLIOGRAPHY

COLLECTOR JIM WELSH DESIRED NEW JOHNSON CITY SONGS

Johnson City Press-Chronicle, July 21, 1950.
Simmons, Moran. "Songs of Appalachia: Music Profiles from the Region."
    http://web.knoxnews.com/special/songs/timeline.html.

RESIDENT'S FIRST AUTOMOBILE RIDE WAS IN AN AMBULANCE

Cox, Bob. *Bowman Family Newsletter*, October 2001; May 2002.
Johnson City Press-Chronicle, April 16, 1947.